Being Woo Woo in an Engineered World

Mary Flanagan Gleason

Life Chronicles Publishing
Give your life a voice!

Life Chronicles Publishing

ISBN 978-1-950649-47-1

Editor: Troy T. Landrum Jr.

All rights reserved

Life Chronicles Publishing

Copyright © 2021 Life Chronicles Publishing

lifechroniclespublishing.com

TABLE OF CONTENTS

Mary Flanagan Gleason

DEDICATION

To my husband, Mark, you are my most persistent nudge and favorite balloon captain. I love you with all my heart. Thank you for taking this journey with me.

To my children, Carrie, Benjamin, and Monica, thank you for leaning into my new way of being. I am grateful you chose me to be your mom.

To my mother, who showed me by example to trust my vision and follow my passions. In your busy life, you always had time for me.

To my father, who always believed in me and in dreams. He shared his ability to communicate beyond this world as well as his gift of welcoming in love wherever he found it.

Mary Flanagan Gleason

ACKNOWLEDGMENTS

There are few successful things I do for which I can take sole credit. This book, in which I share my journey, is no exception. On my journey, I encountered many people who have contributed to my physical, mental, emotional, and spiritual health. In order of appearance: Marilyn Kremen (all of my journals are named Marilyn and I continue to hear your reflective, kind voice), Keesha Ewers, Kristina Bloom, Mary Lee LaBay, Jessica Butts, Debby Handrich, and my many accountability partners over the years.

I am also grateful to my Spirit Guides, Angels, and the many authors who came into my life with Divine timing. I am grateful, too, to my tormentors who showed up as powerful lessons that have shaped me for the better.

I begin each client session with this prayer of gratitude. You may also find it useful to begin your meditations and other conversations with your higher self/higher power.

Thanks to all of the Spirits and Spirit Guides,

Angels and Archangels,

Masters, Teachers and Loved Ones,

Who come today in the highest order of light and love,

With messages that are for my greatest good and highest purpose.

***

"When you are no longer compelled by desire or fear... When you have seen the radiance of eternity in all the forms of time... When you follow your bliss... doors will open where you would not have thought there were doors... and the world will step in and help."

-Joseph Campbell

INTRODUCTION

My journey into the intuitive world brought disruption into every part of my life. This enlightenment rose from the ashes after trying to live into what I thought success was for me. Success that's found in a more orderly (aka Muggle) world.

As I began to understand myself and what it means to be predominantly intuitive, I became aware of so many others who are also struggling against their nature. In my workshops where I share my story, there is always someone who approaches me to say that they are beginning "to know things without the benefit of data." Like me, before understanding my true nature, my clients would express that they couldn't tell anyone because of what others may say or think. This awakening followed by fear is not just my story. It is the story of many others. At this point in my life, I feel compelled to share my story even more broadly. I need to let you know that yes, you can tell others, you must tell others. Thank you for accompanying me on this crazy journey.

According to the Myers Briggs Type Indicator®, only twenty-five percent of us are dominantly intuitive or lead with our sixth sense. Seventy-five percent are dominant sensors; those who, like my husband Mark, experience life primarily through the five senses of touch, taste, sound, sight, and smell. If you are intuitive, there is a significant chance you are in a relationship with a sensor and have experienced some of the cross-wiring I experience with my husband. We are also likely best friends, co-workers, and a part of a family of dominant sensors. The fact that so many people do not get us is not just in your imagination. It does not mean others are not intuitive or that intuitives do not rely on the primary five senses. I am talking about the sixth sense as one's dominant knowing.

For years, I felt stupid. I continuously felt that I had to prove what I knew to others. Why can't I have a mathematical formula to demonstrate what I know? Why do others roll their eyes at me when I make conceptual statements? Most especially, why do my husband and I clash so much? This is my journey into my intelligence, indeed my genius, and how I grew to appreciate how engineered the world is, and why it is so difficult for me to "get it."

My personal reconciling began after a total nervous breakdown which I will share more about in the following sections since it is central to how I came to claim my intuition. On that journey, I learned about the chakras, the seven main energy bodies that live along the spine which carry a tremendous amount of intuition and data by which to live. They became my lifeline, my personal organizer. They give me language, grace, and understanding.

On a Personal Note...

My goal is to reach out to others who are experiencing an awakening to their intuition or are curious to know more about inviting their intuition in. Here you will read a lot about the differences between me, the intuitive, and my husband, Mark, the data-driven, five senses dominant engineer as an illustration of the two worlds we are sometimes caught between. Since it is my book, most things will end in my favor although I keep in mind that someday he may opt to write a rebuttal. Before I get too deep, I just want to say my husband and I have been married for 32 years, have three adult children, two grandchildren, lost three of our parents, loved and said goodbye to three cats, and continue to marvel at the Venn diagram of our lives. Where we overlap is in our love for our family and each other as well as the lessons and respect we brought into the marriage as modeled by our parents who genuinely loved and liked each other. And beer. We overlap in our love of beer.

The Journey

Part I begins with an introduction to the chakras. I was so excited to find them and delve into their wisdom that it seems selfish of me not to share. They will also help you to follow my process. Part II begins at rock bottom. It is where so many worthwhile journeys begin, and I share mine with you here, warts and all, because honesty is key. Part III shares my step-by-step, chakra-by-chakra process to identify and liberate those things that had to go. Part IV describes manifesting a new way of being, something no one could have prepared me for and yet something that felt so right. I knew it to be true. What I share is true, but none of it came as one big chronological progression. I tell you this because it is important to be gentle and patient with yourself as you come into your own alignment. In Part V, I talk about overcoming my fears of being different, and what it means to be married to my opposite: me being an intuitive and he an engineer in an engineered world. That leads to Part VI and the gift of opposition. There is always a gift in resistance, and opposition is the ultimate resistance. Part VII talks about my quest to find scientific evidence of my intuitive skills, still sadly trying to fit in. Spoiler alert: science is still trying to catch up. Proving what I know and what someone else will accept is significantly less important to me now. Finally, in Part VIII, I share some of my great "aha" moments. "Aha" moments are insightful, sometimes scary, and always liberating moments to be embraced.

After each section, I suggest some exercises to help you get comfortable with the material provided and to challenge you to take your own journey. No matter how many times I follow this process, there is always new and rewarding information. I am never done. We are never done.

A Non-Sectarian Word About "Spirit"

Spirit talks to me in ways that encourage, comfort, and challenge me to be better. Some people may have attached a different meaning for

Spirit, perhaps from religious experiences. Please insert the term of your choice: Universe, God, Angel, Higher Power, Higher Self, Nature. They all lead to the same understanding. It is also important to know that being intuitive, communicating with Spirit, is in no way a religion or a conflict with religion. All religions talk about engaging in prayer and meditation to communicate with whatever Higher Power is in keeping with that tradition. I was raised Catholic, and for all my years in the church, I never heard that being psychic or intuitive was an affront to God. Priests, rabbis, imams alike take time to check in with the higher power for guidance. It is not something reserved only for clerics. Occasionally, a potential client is concerned that things I practice, like psychic readings, may conflict with their religion. In that case, I encourage them to check in with their religious leader because I know that it is not. Being in contact with Spirit does not reveal some grand plan, override the need for faith communities, or replace the fellowship we find in temples and churches. Being intuitive is a gift from on high and we all have access to it.

Being Intuitive in an Over Engineered World

Engineers like my husband, Mark, design and make sure that things work properly. Without engineers, the world would be limited in far too many ways. Heaven knows you would not be safe traveling in a car or on a transportation system designed by me. I propose that the reverse is also true. You would not want to live in a house after I tell you that my gut says, "do not buy that house." (That actually happened.)

Mark draws everything out on the nearest pad or cocktail napkin. He is accurate, thorough, and he can do math. He is my opposite. These are his true, authentic gifts and way of being in the world. My story is how I lived and continue to live in the data-driven world the way Mark does before recognizing and living in my own world. As I went through my breakdown and re-emergence, it was not clear that we would still fit together. As I mentioned, we did make it, but I am not the woman he married. Although there were elements of the real me that popped up on occasion as an early warning sign to both of us, I pulled a real switcheroo.

When we were looking for our first home together, we were moving clear across the country for Mark's new job. We were not yet married, had never lived together, were bringing my nine-year-old daughter, I had no job lined up, and everything was scary. If a friend had told me she agreed to this arrangement, I would have said she was crazy to trust some guy so much. Luckily, it turned out to be a good bet, but that first trip to the west coast was huge and scary for all three of us, each in different ways. After looking at numerous houses, we found a newly constructed house that we all liked in a new development. The realtor mentioned that the same floorplan was available down the street and suggested we look before deciding on this lot. Indeed, the second house looked just like the first house, except the closer I got, the harder it was to breathe. When we got to the front door, I did not want to go in. I felt pressure on my head. Mark was embarrassed. "Don't be ridiculous. You have to go in. We need to see if we want to live here." I already knew I didn't, said so, and waited outside. Mark and the realtor rolled their eyes and entered the house along with my daughter. After a few more evil glances and urgings from them, I reluctantly walked through the house and then left taking my daughter with me. For Mark and the realtor, seeing was believing, and I had no tangible evidence. Surely, if something were wrong with the house they would know. Such thinking felt patronizing, but I held my ground, and we bought the first house.

Shortly after the couple who purchased the second house moved in, their upstairs bathtub fell through the family room ceiling. Luckily, they were not home at the time… but I was. I could have been under that tub in that family room had we bought that house. All the reasoning in the world could not have talked me out of that energetic knowing that the house was not built right. I immediately called Mark and the realtor at their offices. I offered a little told-you-so rendition of events. It felt good to claim my highest form of intelligence.

I did not yet know that I was highly intuitive, and over time, I would consistently subjugate my intuition in favor of more "rational" thinking. I called my intuitive moments "hunches," which was acceptable to others even though it sometimes felt more powerful. I find that this act of not owning one's intuition is quite prominent in our society. Far too often, we intuitives have agreed by silent consent to dismiss our knowledge as somehow lesser. Instead, we think there is something wrong with us.

It would take a crisis many years in the making to call my attention to what it means to be intuitive and how important it is for me to live from that perspective. Later I would learn intuitive does not mean I am stupid in this intensely data-driven world. In fact, Forbes magazine talks about intuition as the highest form of intelligence for a business leader. My journey has been long and sometimes lonely, and yet, I was delighted to find so much company once I opened myself to intuition.

Dis-Ease

A doctor may tell you that stomach ulcers are caused by a virus or too much ibuprofen. I don't doubt that, but what happens when neither of those things are true for you, and yet you have five of them? That is what happened to me. Through my study of the chakras, I learned that stomach ulcers, located in the solar plexus chakra, result from leaking personal power. (The solar plexus chakra is your "gut" and the seat of personal power.) You can't hold much power if you're working with a sieve. The only thing I could do was reclaim my power. However, it takes more than words and intentions. A whole lot more. It would take more courage than I could have imagined, first to splay myself wide open to really look at my situation, to own it, and then to live in a new way. Finally, it would take copious amounts of courage and guts to speak my truth to loved ones and others. In short, I risked it all.

My journey to cure my ulcers led me to one very powerful understanding: Nothing happens on one level. We do not get sick on one level, and we cannot heal on one level. The journey to wellness must include physical, mental, emotional, and spiritual aspects. Anything less is a band aid. The chakras helped me find where I was out of alignment, and even more importantly, why. Dis-ease is a life out of alignment.

Mary Flanagan Gleason

Part I

CHAKRAS:
THE MIND-BODY CONNECTION

What are the chakras?

I want to begin by sharing how learning about the chakras was one of the greatest gifts along my journey. The chakras changed the way I thought about my mind/body/spirit/emotion connection. If the chakras were a software app, I would be the lead salesperson.

When I learned about the chakras, they had an incredible organizing effect on my life. This book is not intended to teach you all about the chakras, per se. Rather, they are the handiest way for me to share my journey from overwhelmed to calm, from successful to authentic, from physical and emotional mess to balanced and aligned. Everyone experiences and sorts their life's "aha" moments differently. This is my way. In fact, my chakras have become my most trusted friends. I refer to the chakras throughout this book in hopes that your chakras will be your friends, too. One of the best things about chakra friends is that they only want what is best for you.

Chakra Chart #1 shows the location of the seven main chakras or energy bodies that run from the bottom of the spine or root chakra to the top of the head or crown chakra. They are connected by the sushumna, a channel which works very much like the spinal column carrying messages between chakras. For an excellent introduction to the chakras, I recommend *Chakras for Beginners* by David Pond.

By way of example, the first chakra is always the root at the base of the spine, and they go upward from there. The root carries all that we have made manifest in our life. If you feel too overloaded, that is a sign that the root chakra is calling for attention. In the third illustration, you will see why it is necessary to begin at the root chakra when considering your life and work all the way through to the crown.

Chakra Chart #2: Chakra Meanings shows that each chakra has a particular assignment and so many ways to help you detect and correct imbalances, and most importantly, find your authentic self. Each chakra is associated with a color, gland, organs, sound, crystal, and calls our attention to where things are showing up for us. When out of alignment, a chakra manifests in unhealthy ways. When in alignment, we can call on it to support the other chakras.

Where we feel something in our body is as important as feeling it. It has implications for the cause, and if need be, the cure. All the cough drops in the world will not vanquish a sore throat if the cause is not speaking one's truth.

Chakra Chart #3: Liberating to Manifest, demonstrates how I learned to liberate unwanted things in my life and manifest what would serve me better. Liberating or letting go starts at the base of the spine, the root chakra, which is dense in color and element. With each successive chakra, the element and the color get lighter and lighter. The elements in order are earth, water, fire, air, sound, light and ether. See how everything gets lighter? On the way down, things go from lightest (thought) to densest (real.) Again, this is only meant as an introduction to support your understanding of my journey. For a more thorough explanation, I recommend Anodea Judith's book, *Wheels of Life.*

Knowing the chakras is just the beginning of tapping into your intuition. Knowing what to do with them is key. I use them to assess my life in specific ways. What am I carrying around that I need to let go of? What keeps me too grounded when I need to move forward? How can I ground myself when I feel too unstable?

Chakra Chart #1: Chakra Location

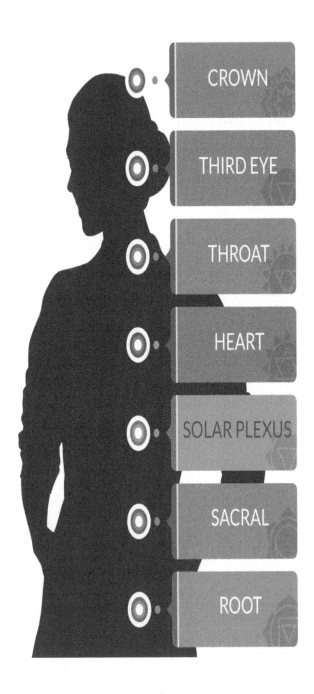

Chakra Chart #2: Chakra Meanings

	1st Root Chakra	2nd Sacral Chakra	3rd Solar Plexus Chakra	4th Heart Chakra	5th Throat Chakra	6th Third Eye Chakra	7th Crown Chakra
Location	Base of Spine	Lower Abdomen	Solar Plexus (stomach)	Heart	Throat	Forehead	Crown
Energy State	Earth Roots Grounding	Water Change Polarities	Fire Power Autonomy	Love Air Breath	Ether Sound Vibration	Light Color Seeing	Consciousness Thought Information
Psychological Function	Survival	Movement	Will	Balance/Love	Communication	Intuition	Knowing
Resulting In	Body Food	Pleasure Emotions	Energy Metabolism	Relationship Affinity	Mantras Telepathy	Visualization/ Imagination Clairvoyance	Understanding Transcendence
Chief Operating Force	Matter/Gravity	Sexuality/ Attraction	Combustion	Unity/Equilibrium	Resonance	Vision	Immanence
Development	Beginning	Nurturance Clairsentience Creation/ Procreation	Transformation Self-Esteem	Healing	Speaking/Listening	Seeing	Knowing/ Meditation
Identity	Physical	Emotional	Ego	Social	Creativity	Architypal	Universal
Body Parts	legs, feet, bones, large intestine, adrenal glands	womb, genitals, kidney, bladder, low back, gonads	digestive system, liver, gall bladder, pancreas, adrenals	lungs, heart, circulatory system, arms, hands, thymus	throat, ears, mouth, shoulders, neck thyroid, parathyroid	eyes, base of skull, brow, pineal	CNS, cerebral cortex, pituitary
Malfunction	obesity, anorexia, sciatica, constipation	sexual problems, urinary trouble	digestive issues, chronic fatigue, hypertension	asthma, coronary and lung disease	sore throat, neck and shoulder pain, thyroid troubles	vision problems, headaches, nightmares	depression, alienation, confusion, inability to learn, apathy
Seed Sound	Lam	Vam	Ram	Yam	Ham	Om	(none)

Mary Flanagan Gleason 2021©

Chakra Chart #3: Liberating to Manifest

Chakra Energy Flow

Manifesting Energy Current

Crown (7th)
Recognize Your Divine Creative Power

Third Eye (6th)
Create a Clear Vision

Throat (5th)
Communicate Your Vision

Heart (4th)
Nurture Love for Vision within Self & Others

Solar Plexus (3rd)
Plan & Take Action

Sacral (2nd)
Enjoy the Journey

Root (1st)
Ground Your Vision into Manifestation

Crown (7th)
Spiritual Awakening

Third Eye (6th)
Intuitive Awareness

Throat (5th)
Open, Authentic Communication

Heart (4th)
Create Healthy Relationships

Solar Plexus (3rd)
Define Ego Identity

Sacral (2nd)
Identify Authentic Desires

Root (1st)
Physical Survival

Liberating Energy Current

Wheels of Life, Anodea Judith

What Does It Mean to Liberate to Manifest?

As I mentioned above, liberating to manifest is the process of letting go of what is in order to make room for what will serve us better. Each time I start at the root and consider the situation. One chakra at a time, all the way to the crown. Once I have gained a sense of release, I can then manifest and welcome into my life what will better serve me. Beginning with the crown all the way through the root.

When I began the process of liberating, I was surprised by what I was holding on to. Some things were deeply subconscious while others I had not considered as holding me back in some negative way. It was as if I went through life as an unwitting collector. If you are like me, you just keep adding to your already full plate, limited calendar, and overstretched finances. At some point, the time comes when you cannot take on one more thing. We try, but it just will not work. Instead, things begin to fall through the cracks.

- Why am I holding on to things the nuns said in third grade?
- Why did I take that job when I knew it was not a good fit for me?
- Why didn't I speak up sooner about things in relationships that left me feeling wounded?
- When will I learn that "no" is a complete sentence?

Just like cleaning out a closet, we shake our heads, wondering why we are still holding on to things we no longer need, or that no longer fit, or completely forgot we had. But there they are, taking up space, lying in wait, draining our resources. For me, I had to look at several things:

- Like certain friendships that no longer brought me joy, or returned favors, or who laid their problems at my feet.
- Like the constant demands of climbing the success ladder in a career I no longer loved.
- Like Mark's insatiable need for more details that I no longer even tried to provide.

We have the option to pick it all up, neaten the pile, to keep stuffing things in the closet, or to take stock, decide what to keep, what to toss, what to pass along, and what to give back to its rightful owner. It is a very liberating act that really must happen to make room for those things that are more important and will serve us better. It is also an act of bravery.

Christopher Robin Explains

The 2018 movie, Christopher Robin, is the perfect example of when one engages in liberating and manifesting. It is based on the character Christopher Robin in Winnie the Pooh. The adult version of this once little boy with wonderful imaginary friends and creator of copious adventures finds himself rather unplayful. His children are hungry for their dad to find time to be in their world. After much resistance, Christopher Robin realizes that he has grown into a serious bureaucrat and has buried his ability to enjoy life somewhere at the bottom of his briefcase. This is where his liberating journey begins.

First, Christopher realizes that his life is not working for him. He has manifested far too much seriousness and great distance from his family (root.) We watch as he recognizes that he has lost the art of joy (sacral), felt powerless in his present circumstances (solar plexus), is out of alignment with his true passions and relationship with others (heart), gives voice to his unhappiness (throat), sees his life for what it is (third eye), and releases it in frustration (crown).

Having created immense space in his life, it is time for renewal, to manifest a better way of life. First, he takes responsibility for creating his own joy (crown), envisions his old way of life and how to make it part of his reality now (third eye), invites his children to join him (throat), reconnects with his old childhood friends and includes his children on the adventure (heart), feels empowered by what he used to know (solar plexus), finds incredible joy as he rescues his old pals from the stream (sacral), and resettles into a happier way of life (root.)

I promise you, once you know the chakras, you will see them reflected everywhere.

My Experience

Like the adult Christopher Robin, my life was not working for me. Hard as I tried to handle it all and push through, it just was not working. I called on all the lessons I had learned early in life: work

9

harder, be smarter, show up, handle it. As a young child, around six or seven years old, I remember my father worked three jobs. He was the postman by day, walking a twelve-mile route. In the wee hours of the morning, he delivered newspapers to rural areas. On Sundays and occasional evenings, he worked as a housefather at a juvenile detention center. My mother worked as a nurse, spending all day on her feet. Whenever possible, she took on private duty shifts to earn extra money, plus it provided her with quiet time to do her homework as she was putting herself through college. The model for survival and success was on display for me every day. In my family, it was a compliment of the highest degree to be considered a hard worker.

When I was nineteen, I had my first child. When my daughter was an infant, I enrolled in business courses and earned a diploma as a medical office assistant. It was a nine-month course that allowed me to secure a full-time job with benefits and career opportunities. The best benefit was free college courses which I took at night. It would not take me long to realize that I could not keep up with the students who came from private prep schools and for whom this prestigious college was their second choice after being wait-listed by the Ivy League schools. They were well prepared for college, studied in groups, and existed with a genuine sense of entitlement. Even though they were my age peers, we had nothing in common.

A seemingly small but telling incident happened in one of my evening classes. One student nudged her friends, pointed at me, and they all laughed. It was my jeans, probably from JC Penney's, but definitely not Jordache, the elites' label of the day. I am not sure what reaction they were expecting, but I am fairly sure it was not the one they got. I very proudly replied that "at least I paid for them myself, without daddy's gold card." My parents would have been proud of me. I knew that I was a hard worker and that was the most important thing. It was also my first lesson that no one can make me feel shame without my permission. By the age of 21, I had my own apartment, was raising my daughter (with love and support from my family), and on my way to my first promotion. Working, earning, and being recognized were their own rewards. They were the core elements of success as demonstrated by my parents.

Many years later, I found myself in an overwhelming situation. Still, the old story that working harder will take care of whatever comes my way played on as if it were still relevant. My husband worked in global sales for several high-tech companies in the 1990s-2000s. At that time, companies were being bought and sold as quickly as possible without regard to employees. It was a dog-eat-dog environment, and he was burned out. We had two more children by then and Mark's being on the road all the time meant little time with us.

Contrary to the companies and organizations our parents had worked for, these start-up company founders planned their exit strategies as part of their earliest business plans. Not all of them wanted to be the next Microsoft or Amazon. They wanted to sell their new business to them at a huge profit and close the doors. Gone were the days when you worked in a lifetime contract with an employer: you stayed, and they rewarded you with things like pensions. The impact this approach had on employees was abysmal. This told me volumes about my husband's world.

Of course, we hoped one of those companies would hit it big, and we would be rich, but that was not what the cards held for us. One company that Mark had been working for eight years sold to new investors who drained all the employees' knowledge and then laid them off. During that time, his layoff was just what he needed: a respite, a chance to catch his breath. A year and a half later, he found a new job doing the same thing – high tech sales. Still, dog-eat-dog environment but on a little sturdier ground, or so we thought. After fifteen months, he came home one day and announced that the office was closed. The company had been found guilty of stealing the source code for the software product Mark was selling. We had just regained our financial footing, and here we were again, back at square one. Meanwhile, I had a pressure cooker job that I lost, and we overlapped with unemployment for eleven months. This second round of his unemployment felt different to me. In my mind, he already had a chance to rest and renew. Why was he not eagerly looking for another job? Why was the garden so perfect, and the kids always off with him on an adventure? It was my counselor who pointed out to me that Mark might have been experiencing some level of depression. He had never had to really look for a job. He had multiple offers coming out of college and was recruited for successive positions ever since. Mark, being unemployed twice, was not something he anticipated ever having to work through. He, too, was raised with a strong work ethic and a firm belief that education meant never being unemployed. So many instilled values no longer holding and guiding him.

About that time, I jumped back into working with a former employer for about a year and then took the job that I should never have taken. Why? Because it paid more. When you work in the nonprofit sector as I did, you better align with the mission, and this time I was not. I just needed the money. No matter where I worked, I was still making less than half of what Mark earned, and his salary is the one we built our lives around. I needed help but I did not ask for it. I believed that if I worked just a little harder, it would all be okay. If I complained to Mark about his job search efforts, I feared being a nag. After a particularly awful day, one where I just knew I could no longer do this. I came home and announced, "I'm quitting my job! I hate it! I don't know who I am when I'm there, and my stomach really hurts!" I think I said something snarky or equally unhelpful like "unemployment seems to be working for you, so I thought I'd give it a try." It was one of those signs showing me that I was about to erupt but not quite yet.

It was only a few months later that Mark started his new position. He found the job after finally voicing the kind of job and type of company he did want to work for - his big positive-manifesting moment. I knew then that we would be okay, even if not for a very long while. This is when I could fully let go and hit bottom. When I could admit to myself that I could not do it all and working harder was not the answer. I described myself harshly as a failure and stupid and comforted myself with a lot of victim-y thoughts. I did a whole lot of blaming, especially Mark. But I would grow to learn that I was misaligned with my true self. Nothing more. Nothing less.

I had hit bottom before with past bouts of reactionary depression – times when the rug was pulled out from underneath me - and got back up, but this time was different. This time, I did not want to get back to the way things were. I wanted different, better, even though I did not know yet what that was. All I knew was whatever I was doing had to stop. I trusted that something new would emerge, and it did.

Excellence and Genius

In every facet of life, we must first liberate what no longer works to make room for the things that work. Identifying the specific parts that are not working is imperative. I started by looking at what was in my life, one big chunk or small piece at a time. What would take me a long time to figure out is that my work with nonprofits is what Gay Hendricks, author of The Big Leap, would call my "zone of

14

excellence." The zone of excellence is where you are so well-versed, you can do it all day long with your eyes closed. For some, it is a great place to live out one's career. For me, I hit what Hendricks called the "upper limit problem." I needed to find an even better way to show up in the world. I needed to make the next big leap into my "zone of genius."

No longer being on staff made me happy. The politics alone were enough to make me call in sick. That is when I began consulting. I felt secure in what I knew and validated when sharing it with other organizations. It aligned me with my best self, the ability to see the big picture, to pull the disparate pieces together to create a higher-level of understanding. Later, I would find out that this sort of big picture viewing that sees how one area is impacting another is a critical trait of being intuitive. Unfortunately, when you are on staff, no one wants to hear it. When you are a consultant, they pay you to say it. As much as I found some relief here, there still had to be more. It would take a while longer until I would discover my "zone of genius." In the same book, Hendricks says the zone of genius is where we really shine. It is where we make the biggest leap of all. Genius is where we are aware of our true gifts with every fiber of our being. Just reading that description struck a deep chord and crowning "aha" moment: Intuition is my zone of genius! It is my genius, and I have ignored it, discounted its value, believing excellence was as good as it gets. One can certainly bring their genius into their excellence but first I had to know what my genius was and how to use it. Eventually, this would lead to my becoming an executive intuition coach where leaders learn how to call on their intuition in everyday business. Once I locked into my zone of genius, I was amazed at how quickly Spirit/Universe puts opportunities to excel on your path.

During this time of liberation, I had to also consider my friends. Some were fun for a while but no longer brought me joy, or I had to do too much of the work, or I no longer agreed to participate in their dramas. Liberating myself from other people's dramas was a biggie because it had been a wonderful place to hide from my own life. Even closer to home, Mark required an exactness from life that I just do not share and could not deliver. That was the kind of thing I would take on and then not do well. That triggered shame, woe-is-me, stupid self-talk that ate away at my personal power and left me feeling angry at everyone, especially Mark. I had to let go of my victim/martyr story that somehow, it is my job to save the whole world, and if it doesn't work out then I am a failure.

My parents demonstrated the incredible work ethic that I integrated into my way of life, but I did so in ways that no longer worked for me. I would grow to thank my mother and father for their remarkable example and find my limits within their values. My mind was filled with false beliefs, with loads of shoulds and oughts, all of which needed to be released. This was not a one-time task. It took many passes, and still occasionally, they resurface. The difference is that now I am more aware of those thoughts. Tell-tale phrases like "I can handle it" still flow through my mind and now I know how to pay close attention when I catch myself thinking it: what is it I am saying about this issue before me? Is it true? Should I be handling it? I have dozens of examples, and please know that I have done my best to share many of them with you throughout the liberating section below. I just want to note that as these realizations came to me, not once did my mother ever shame or criticize. My need to please was my own expectation.

Exercise 1:

Start a fresh journal for the exercises contained in this book. Keep it as a separate accounting of how to sort through your thoughts and experiences in the specific ways outlined here.

1. Begin by documenting your story. What is happening for you right now? Where are you feeling good, and where are you feeling stuck, hesitant, or confused?
2. Dig deeper into how things got to be where they are, be they positive or negative. Be as descriptive as possible.
3. When you're done writing, notice the tone of the words you use and how they make you feel.

The next series of exercises suggest ways to help you sort through different areas of your life by heightening your intuition and connection with your higher self. For now, just jotting them down on paper is helpful.

Mary Flanagan Gleason

Part II:

HITTING ROCK BOTTOM

The problem with problems is that we never know where the bottom is. We spend so much time just trying to put one foot in front of the other that we do not think to take a step back to get a broader perspective. We go into survival mode where the focus narrows to the next immediate need. We dare not look up. We just redefine success.

Finding Bottom

All the while my stomach was begging me to pay attention to the self-harm I was inflicting, two things finally got my attention. The first was the test results that showed I had five stomach ulcers. The second was the inadequate treatment offered. Had I stuck with the Western-prescribed therapies, I have no doubt I would be dead. No one talked to me about looking at the whole picture – lifestyle, eating habits, depression. I was told to just keep taking more antacids as if there were no side effects. But there are side effects, and the treatment was not helping to heal the ulcers. Taking antacids in any amount did not address how the ulcers got there in the first place. The doctor said that only two things cause stomach ulcers: a virus for which I tested negative or too much Ibuprofen. When I mentioned that neither applied to me, the doctor assumed I was not being honest. But I knew the answer: everything had to change. I had to quit. Everything. Food, job, career advancement, everything. And find alternative treatments.

Before I got sick, before the stomach ulcers, and the nervous breakdown, I had been running frantically trying to be all things to all people and telling myself, "I can handle it." I absolutely hated my job, had made a lot of decisions based on external things such as a bigger house or better salary, and had become enslaved by the life I thought I wanted. Finally, with few choices left, I had to stop everything. Even though my family really needed me to work, I quit my job, gave up food because it was literally killing me to eat, and hunkered down into a rare silence. This was my bottom. Now the only way to go was up, but it would be a slow climb with a few zigzags. If I were a baseball team, you would say I was entering a rebuilding year.

Beginning the Ascent

About this time, a friend opened a clinic offering Ayurvedic medicine or functional medicine approach to health. It was here that my conscious journey into the intuitive realm began. "Nothing," my practitioner told me, "happens on one level. We do not get sick on just one level, so we cannot heal on just one level." This is when I would learn about the chakras, starting with the solar plexus or gut. It is the center of our personal power, and mine was leaking everywhere. To heal, to reclaim my power, I had to be a full participant in my treatment by observing a very restrictive diet, ingest a regimen of needed dietary supplements, and engage in a sincere and consistent meditation practice. Learning about the chakras would lead to my understanding of how to live a well-balanced life.

Very quickly, I became immersed in my world in a new way. I experienced intense realizations and gained information that was equally empowering and isolating: Empowering because I could see, hear, and know so much just by sitting in the silence where my Spirit guides and angels were waiting for me, happy to finally have my undivided attention. Isolating because this information was not anything anyone else in my immediate life could relate to. I felt alone with dynamic, life-altering information and in desperate need of community. Eventually, community would come in many different ways from many surprise avenues. But not yet.

Finding Community

In one meditation, I requested guidance to find a supportive and educated community. My Spirit guide literally said, "meetup." So, I went to the computer, clicked on Meetup.com, and searched for psychic development. I could not believe how many sites came up in my area! "Wow! I'm not alone." Then I felt incredibly overwhelmed by the number of choices, and once again, I heard a gentle voice say, "keep scrolling." So, I did until I heard "stop." It landed on a six-week course called Intuitive You! ™. I paid my $100, and that following week I went to an eclectic gathering of people whose paths I may never have otherwise crossed. The first thing the instructor asked me is, "why are you here?" I said that I wanted to know if I was psychic. She very gently smiled and said, "Oh my, yes. Your energy is huge. Let's get you some ways to understand and control it." I melted into the chair, never wanting to leave. Sweet relief and acceptance were mine.

If any of this resonates with you, I hope this book will become part of your community. Among the many things I explored with various groups was the Myers Briggs Type Indicator, the Enneagram, and meditation practices. Each led me to a deeper understanding, and a greater appreciation of me which I came to learn is where all the deep and important work lies.

I am so grateful that I continued to find additional teachers along the way who seemed to show up with the Divine timing I have come to rely on. That Intuitive You! ™ six-week course extended into a two-year journey with the same instructor. She introduced me to whole new worlds and ways to explore them. A deeper dive into the chakras was just the beginning. We explored astral travel, past life regression, manifesting, channeling, mediumship (talking with souls that have passed), intuitive tools like tarot, divination rods, crystals, pendulums, and understanding the various ways intuition shows up for each person. Intuitive You!™ is now a book referenced in the bibliography at the end of this book.

It was the past life experiences that led me to a different instructor that came with a community of equally curious souls. This led me to study hypnotherapy.

To learn how to retrieve past lives and which, in turn, led me to whole new worlds of understanding and ways to experience life and ways to help others. There were more experiences, but you get the idea. I felt a deep sense of knowing that I was in the right place. I had a distinct recognition that "this is what 'home' feels like to my soul." It is more expansive than contracting. I just knew there was more outside of what I saw, and now I had others who also knew. All these teachings felt downright normal to me.

While my new normal was emerging, the dissonance between me and the engineered Muggle world grew. Mark could not find the old me, nor did he wish to grow with me in this way. Since we can never change another, my hope was that he would become at least a little curious. No matter his response, it was clear that my Genie was not going to go timidly back in the bottle, and I would no longer attempt to make it do so.

Eventually, all my learnings about me had to circle back to my immediate family, most notably my engineer husband. He was supportive while also at a loss with me, this physical mess of enlightenment. And, because my earliest insights and learnings happened over several years, we had to keep revisiting the same territory with new insights. Mark's goal was for me to get better so we could get back to "normal." Hard to argue with except that I had a new normal that was ill-defined and almost without language, which, of course, is not within the engineer's primary realm of discernment. I use my relationship with Mark and his engineering approach to life to demonstrate the resistance I met and how important it was to my growth. You may relate to this with a different relationship or situation.

Exercise 2:

Think of one or more situations you feel you are fighting against. Perhaps it is a job or a relationship that simply will not change despite your best efforts.

1. Think of each situation, one at a time. Notice where you feel it in your body, which chakra. Consult Chakra Chart #2 and note which chakra and its meaning is impacted.
2. Notice how it feels. Is it expansive, contracting, painful, emotional, sorrowful?
3. Listen to the words you use to describe the situation. Are they blaming, shaming, or otherwise harmful thoughts?

Be sure to write this down and be prepared to call on them for upcoming exercises.

P.S. Two people can have the same experience and experience it in different ways. It is not helpful to ever compare yourself to another.

Part III:

ONE MUST LIBERATE TO MANIFEST

Liberating from the Bottom Up

To rid myself of what no longer serves me, I learned to start at the root chakra at the base of the spine and consider each aspect through the next chakra, and the next until I reached the crown. I did not realize it then, but I had a rehearsal of this many years before when I worked with a therapist, Kathy.

Kathy was particularly struck by my paralyzing efforts to buy clothes. I was young, outgoing, and had a cute figure. Mine was not a body image issue. Still, I picked out clothes that were usually too big and often the wrong color. She asked me to close my eyes and walk her through my most recent dressing room experience. I recalled bringing in tons of clothes, in various styles and colors and leaving with nothing. Then she asked me to recount my thought process as I tried each one on. Wow! What an eye-opener to say these things aloud, to give conscious voice to my thought process. In the process I was overwhelmed with competing opinions from my husband who wanted me to look sexier ("You dress like an old lady"), from my mother who valued practicality above all else ("It should be washable and something you can wear for several years"), and, of course modesty, to the nuns who made it clear that you are a sinner if you cause others to think bad thoughts ("You girls go around asking for it and then you want sympathy.") I opened my eyes. It was impossible to reconcile wanting my husband to find me sexy, my mother to find my choices practical, and the nuns to just get off my back. Kathy was silently nodding, feeling the overwhelm. Finally, she spoke: "My, what a crowded dressing room."

We then spent time visually escorting each voice out of the dressing room and welcomed in occasions. Where would I be wearing these garments? Work, date night, children's school events, etc. Then I could begin to devise my own definitions of what was appropriate. Thinking back on it, Kathy guided me through liberating to manifesting in one hour.

Recalling that experience with Kathy helped me to recognize what I could accomplish with this line of inquiry and contemplation. I chuckled when I realized that the chakra color scheme was the same as we learned in kindergarten - ROY-G-BIV – red, orange, yellow, green, blue, indigo, violet. Funny I should circle back to elementary learning right as my life called for me to hit reset.

Like the dressing room exercise, liberating, freeing up space, and offloading useless and counterproductive thinking, would require that I take an honest look at what was not working or no longer served me and releasing it from my reality. Some obvious big chunks needed to go such as my job, certain friendships, and negative self-talk. And as I peeled back the proverbial onion layers, I realized there were some smaller, less obvious things that also held me back like, being cynical and sarcastic. Cynicism required that I always be on the alert for who is trying to take advantage of me, while sarcasm was a way to dismiss attempts at sincerity. There were other things that needed to go, too, like my fears that others are always judging me and my old definition of success – a bigger house, the next promotion, etc. Fifteen years later, I continue to embrace this process because of its powerful insights and rewards. As I released situations, relationships, and thoughts that kept me too closely grounded, unable to move, I could feel space opening inside of me. There was a lightness of being that made me feel like a carefree child. There was a big realization that I was not obligated to any of them. Giving myself over to other people's opinions and expectations meant giving over control of my life and my happiness to others. I was ready to decide what I wanted to wear. Sounds silly, but really, it was huge.

Once I learned how to liberate, I then learned how to manifest a more desirable life to fill the space I had freed up. I did not want to use the same mindset to create my new life. Examining the mindset is the crux of any inward journey since our thoughts create our reality. There were few quick and easy answers because each had to be examined through the lens of what purpose each was serving and then I had to address that purpose. When I quit smoking many years earlier with the help of self-hypnosis, I realized I used cigarettes as a literal smokescreen with my then boss. That was back when smoking in the workplace was still considered a cultural norm. She was constantly barging in with the next ill-thought-out request, but she would not enter my office if I were smoking. Part of quitting smoking had to include a more productive way of discouraging my boss's constant interruptions.

This is what I had to do now – find the real reason why things are the way they are -- only the questions were even more grave. I had to get clear about what would make me happy and how I would take responsibility for providing it. It required becoming one hundred percent responsible for everything in my life.

The Root Cause

The Root Chakra: Physical Survival

Color Red, Element is earth, located at the base of the spine. In charge of: Basic needs, safety, legs, grounding.

The root chakra keeps us grounded. Its first concern is physical safety. If you do not have all the basic needs of life, then you are unsafe and nothing else matters until you meet those basic needs. When out of alignment, we find it hard to get out of bed, we feel weighed down, we may be constipated, overweight, fearful, in need of food, clothing or shelter. We may be stuck with someone or something that makes it impossible to move the way we want. When out of alignment, the root chakra is often filled with fear.

The Healing Process Begins

To begin the healing process, I had to take a meditative journey to see what was here at the base. The root serves as the ballast or anchor. When I looked at the basis of my problems, what I had manifested, I found a lot of false beliefs about me and about how life ought to go. False beliefs about what I was capable of, in a limiting and unbalanced way, and all the things I had attracted into my world and could no longer handle. One of my first "aha" moments was "no more promotions, please!" That was quickly followed by no more friends who drain me with their negativity and unresolved issues. No more people who need rescuing – most especially me.

When I closed my eyes to envision this ruby red glowing disc of energy, I was shocked to find that it was such a dark shade of red it was almost black. The energy contained in the root chakra was sluggish and felt very much like an anchor holding me under. I was being weighed down by all I had manifested: a job I never really wanted, a house that became too expensive, the belief that I should not get mad at my husband during long bouts of unemployment. I would later learn how much of that manifesting happened through my thoughts and beliefs, but I will talk more about that when I get to the upper chakras.

I also met a Spirit Guide who seemed to dwell in this chakra, a Native American, named Pokjum. (I have often heard the criticism that everyone has a native Spirit Guide. Saying that someone has one somehow makes it seem phony. In my experience, we all have at least one because we take in the Spirit vibration from Mother Earth. Wherever we walk, the ancestral spirit of the land will guide us (if we allow for it). Spirit Guides are wise souls not in a physical form. Some are with me always, while others pop in depending on the occasion. Frequently, Spirit Guides give themselves a physical appearance to help connect with their purpose and message. Some may call them angels or other non-physical presences. I always question their mission before accepting their guidance because I want to ensure their purity, that they really are spirits of the highest order of light and love and not something with lesser intents. Connecting with the spirit realm without a healthy amount of skepticism can leave me open to unwanted influences. Not every person is pure, nor is every spirit looking to make good in the world.

Pokjum watched me skirt through the meditative forest I had visualized for weeks, trying to bypass him and whatever it was he wanted from me. He was patient and ever-present. Finally, I engaged him. He wanted me to sit down. There was a clearing for one tree in this massive forest, and he wanted me to sit in that exact spot. When I eventually surrendered to this request, I visualized myself sitting and instantly began growing roots from the base of my spine that went unbelievably deep into the ground. They were strong and powerful and took me on the most incredible journey. I could go anywhere I wanted. Anywhere! I could travel to other trees and easily visualized their communication system. My roots would stretch out and break the surface, climbing the tallest trees for new perspectives and experiences. It was nothing shy of amazing.

When it was time for me to return to consciousness, I sobbed as I realized how I had never really put down roots in my life for fear that I would be tethered in unwanted ways or sure that something better existed elsewhere. I was always ready for the next experience without having taken advantage of the one before me. Pokjum showed me how important roots are, especially if I wanted to sprout wings. As the hymn goes, "Roots hold me close; wings set me free." Putting down those roots helped me for what was to come next. It was not roots that held me back but my thoughts about what success is and things like a bigger house and having more "stuff" that held me down. There is a difference between being rooted in place and being bogged down by heavy things. The latter is more debilitating than grounding.

Further examination required that I take a good long look at what was in my life that I no longer wanted or needed or could tolerate. It was a long list and just calling it out made me feel lighter.

I could not just walk away from everything, but some were easier to dismiss than I had imagined. Once I identified my prime objective -- to live into what serves my greatest good and highest purpose -- the needy, clingy, draining people were gone either through outright conversations or by simply no longer engaging with them. Funny how many of those people never called to see how I was doing which I did for them all the time. It is tempting to feel like someone who was taken advantage of but, in truth, I allowed it if not welcomed it. If I am honest with myself, I sometimes even sought them out because solving other people's problems allowed me to run from my own issues. I would later learn to "stay on my side of the net." That rescuing others tendency was my nurture, not my nature.

I grew up in the shadow of the bumper sticker motto, "if you're not a part of the solution, you're a part of the problem," which I interpreted to mean that it was up to me to solve all problems – mine and everybody else's. I also grew up in the shadow of my mother, a nurse, who extended family members dubbed "a saint." My two brothers both grew up to become police officers, one of which also became a volunteer firefighter and EMT. One might say that rescuing others was also a family value.

There are also things that I did not want to liberate myself completely from, like the friends who did show up. They sent a card, some flowers, called to check in, etc. Still, many things needed some cleaning up, repositioning, rectifying, if they were going to stay. Things like my spouse. Spouses are more than a Marie Kondo project of the simple test, "does this bring me joy?" It is a long and painful conversation first with yourself of what you are willing to risk in favor of the honest conversation about what you need going forward. Did I even know what I needed? That was and is an ever-evolving concept, but I had to work with where I was as I was experiencing it. So, I started the conversation with Mark very honestly: "I'm changing. You have done nothing wrong, and I don't know what this means for me. I am working on how I want to respond to life without the usual sarcasm and cynicism. I'm sure it looks like I'm no fun anymore." The truth is that when enlightenment starts, that Knowing Genie only continues to grow and call to you more loudly. It is best to address it openly or you'll tire as I did from stuffing it down and growing resentful of others without explanation. Then I had to continue to explore my own motivations, continue dialoguing with my husband, and let go of what he might do with this information. He gets to make choices for himself, too. All of it felt obvious. None of it was easy.

If you do not feel safe, you cannot do this work. Thankfully, my husband is not an abusive man. While our marriage hits rough patches from time to time, there was no reason for me to feel physically or psychologically unsafe. I just want to take that off the table because if you are in an unsafe situation, understand you cannot change another, and it is imperative to first find safety.

When I began my sorting, the heaviest objects of all were my thoughts and beliefs, many of which I didn't even know I was harboring. I had grown attached to those things, so I had to weigh the righteous indignation of having created them against the limits each

33

imposed. When I was learning to drive, I would argue that something might be the other driver's fault and, my father would say, "Being right is good. But what good is being dead right." The time had come for me to let go of being right because I did not want to have to admit that I made mistakes in my approach to work, in my relationships, in just about every area of my life. It took months of working on balancing the chakras. Gradually, the flecks of manifested negatives began to fall away and gradually exposed the beautiful ruby red energy of my root chakra. I continue to go through the review, the balancing, and the conversations many times to keep my life moving forward. These first few years of practice, though, were a doozy. I was a woe-is-me victim, and it was not pretty. If I am not the victim, then it means no one else is responsible for my unhappiness or much less fixing it. My life was my responsibility, one hundred percent. As Winnie the Pooh would say, "such bother."

The Sacral Chakra: Identify Authentic Desires
Color: Orange. Element: Water. Location: Just below the navel. In Charge of: Emotions/ Pleasure/ Reproductive Organs/Bladder/ Kidneys /Colon and Smell

The sacral chakra water oversees the flow of softening the earth below and tempering the fire in the solar plexus above. The Sacral chakra is the center of creativity and pleasure. If the sacral is not working correctly, one can develop issues with the bladder, kidneys, colon, or reproductive organs. Energy such as unresolved anger can cause this. One gets literally pissed off or blocked up when not living in the flow. The sacral chakra is also essential to our creativity, including procreation and giving birth to new ideas. It co-creates with the throat chakra.

Does this bring me joy?

The reproductive organs are connected with this second chakra. It wants us to feel positively orgasmic about life. When I meditated to look at this next step toward liberating my dis-ease, I found murky brown, sludge-like water, instead of beautiful orange energy. It was shapeless and filled with floating pieces of broken furniture. At least that's what I saw in my mind's eye. I had no idea yet what the broken furniture meant, but it was preventing the water from flowing. It was not a place for creativity and pleasure to thrive. There was no easily spinning, orange glowing disc - what a mess. I could not change my life without first cleaning up this mess.

What is broken furniture doing in my sacrum?

Why am I hanging on to it?

Who could help me?

My journal pages were filling up fast!

It is worth mentioning that with all my intensely focused meditations, I found a different Spirit Guide residing in each chakra except for the sacral and the throat, the chakra that co-create. Both

35

were being guided by what presented itself as "Mr. Conductor," like an orchestra conductor. As I worked and worked over many months to brighten the waters and regain the flow, I found the furniture reassembled itself as orchestra stands and chairs, each filled with talented musicians who played beautiful waltzes and made me feel light on my feet.

Again, this was over a long period of time, but the effects of working in this realm began to make a difference almost immediately. Floating in the murky waters was pure crap. Literally. It was all the nonsense I had retained, much of which did not even belong to me. Starting with energetic nets for scooping and building up to opening large sewer drains, I visualized running the waters through repeatedly until the crap was gone and the waters could flow once again. Yet, simply removing the crap was not enough. For real insight, I had to look at how this crap got there in the first place.

The question I started with was, "who thought it was a good idea to give this crap to me," but I was still in my victim thinking and tried to blame others. Getting mad at my mother or the nuns or whoever else put notions in my head was futile. Whatever my mother shared with me, it was still up to me to determine the truth and motivation for its role in my life, like the rescuing thing. My mother is a deeply thoughtful person who found pleasure in helping others. Nursing was her nature. From that I can pick the lessons of caring, of being sympathetic, of showing concern. Looking back, I realize mom was very careful to show compassion without taking on others' issues. It was me who interpreted such gestures that I somehow needed to resolve other's problems. That's on me. As time went on, I learned how much I had accepted carrying others' burdens although I was never asked to do so. As I pulled away, I also saw how many people either did not care – like no one ever asked me anyway - or were upset because my care had become an entitlement in their life. It was not a graceful period.

Explaining all of this to my engineer husband who tried his best to support was getting harder and harder. These experiences were so powerful, but they distanced me from a loving relationship. While Mark required data, I only had visions and concepts to offer that mostly came without the benefit of language. From the outside, I looked idle and raggedy but inside myself everything was on the move.

Just to review; for this one chakra alone (and there were still five more to go!) I had to-

- o Understand the chakra's power and identify what a healthy sacrum looked like energetically
- o What did it look like for me?
- o Why did it look that way?
- o What was I going to do with all that crap?
- o How was I going to change and stop taking on crap?
- o What was I willing to change (think victim story)?
- o How could I forgive myself for allowing this to happen?

- o How would I act going forward?
- o How the hell was I ever going to explain what was happening to me to anyone else?

That last one turned out to be best answered by acknowledging my own confusion, promising to keep loved ones appropriately informed, recognize that this was not going to be easy, and ask them to be gentle in their feedback.

Solar Plexus: Define Ego

Color: Yellow. Element: Fire. Location: Stomach. In charge of Personal Power/ Stomach/Intestines/Digestion

The Solar Plexus is all about personal power, living our truth, and not letting others' opinions dictate what we know to be true for us. It is literally how we digest life. When it is out of alignment, we suffer things like stomach ulcers, low self-esteem, become vulnerable to bullies, unable to engage the heart chakra above in a healthy way. We often default to woe-is-me thinking or victimhood, or even fiery rage. It is how we put this fire to use in matters.

Murky Water is Useless with Fire

When it came time to look at my solar plexus, the third chakra, I found out how important it is to have free-flowing water from below. The solar plexus element is fire and as I mentioned before, it is the center of personal power and self-love. If it is out of order, then there is no way we are living in right relation with others (heart) or can hear the messages of a higher calling (upper chakras.) My solar plexus was beyond bright yellow, and the energy was not a neatly spinning disk but a shapeless mass that expanded much too far from the core of my body. It was so hot it burned to think about, and of course, this is where the five ulcers appeared. I burned five holes in my stomach before Spirit finally got my attention. More pleasant thoughts that flow from the sacral waters can help put the fire out, but my water wasn't flowing, and I was eating myself alive with heat and a terribly limiting belief: I can handle it – whatever it is. Total ego and totally false. Even if I could do it all, I shouldn't.

Working with a homeless shelter for youth and young adults years later, I would hear repeatedly from these young people that they didn't need anybody. They could handle everything by themselves. They were so proud of being completely self-sufficient, except, of course, for the need for food and shelter. When we feel powerless, the ego tells us that we are more powerful than is true and that asking for help is a sign of weakness. We just have to redefine success.

The delusion of complete self-sufficiency is where the real problems lie. As I started to ask for help, Mark teased me, calling me high maintenance. "What would low maintenance look like, I wondered?" I cannot help but think it might look like Ted Kaczynski, the Unabomber and American terrorist who lived off the grid with almost no human contact and sent letter bombs to capitalists he perceived were ruining the world. Living all alone, yet believing it was his job to change the world. The rest of us are high maintenance, and our most demanding client is self. Mark was not refusing to help me; he just wasn't used to these types of requests, plus I was already a melted puddle of emotions. He had to pick up a lot more with the kids and the house. My container for personal power was unable to hold so much as a morsel of personal fortitude. It was around this time I would come to loathe a commercial lingo from my formative years, "I can bring home the bacon, fry it up in a pan, and never let you forget you're a man." Damaged bodies go hand in hand with damaging beliefs.

Here I received a powerful message while in a meditative trance. A Spirit Guide who called herself Najja, showed herself to me. She was a very powerful presence wearing a beautifully colored Indian sari. I liken her to the tarot card, the Queen of Wands. Like the Queen of Wands, Najja is very much in charge of where she puts her energy. She said little to me except, "it's time to clean this up." She added, "I am you. You know how to do this and how to be me." Now I will sometimes call on her in the middle of the day to think, "What would Najja do?" Often, I will feel a nudge pushing me toward the incredibly obvious.

Mark helplessly watched while I struggled with this realization because he did not understand it and knew he could not do any of this work for me. Like so many men and logical thinkers, Mark is a fixer, and this did not call on any of his best skills. My illness made him feel bad. My journey made him feel lost. My journey made us feel separate. Before I could rebuild us, I needed to build the new me first. I needed to let go of false beliefs, unrealistic expectations of myself, and the proper way to ask for help. Insights into my own power were scary, like learning to fly a plane or drive a car -- freedom and responsibility in one shared experience.

Heart Chakra: Create Healthy Relationships

Color: Emerald Green. Element: Air. Location: Center of the chest. In charge of Heart, Lungs, Arms

This chakra resides in the center of the chest. When in alignment, it allows blood to flow throughout the body, and it is easy for us to breathe. When out of alignment, we experience anxiety and can develop heart disease or pneumonia. Air feeds the fire and our passions. It is how we are in relationship with other people and situations. It connects the lower three chakras to the upper chakras. If the heart is not in right relation to a situation or person, it is difficult to find new solutions until the relationship is liberated.

The Heart of the Matter

Now I would have told you that I was a good mother and a good wife through this entire nervous breakdown. But how is that possible when I wasn't in right relation with myself? No, it was more like meeting minimum standards with fake smiles, quick to anger, a severed connection to career, and the overwhelming demands of

41

everyday life that kept me on a slowing gerbil wheel, having long ago reached the point of diminishing returns. My kids will tell you that I was mean. They did not want to talk to me because I would snap. My husband overcompensated for the mean mommy while comforting himself that soon I would be back to "normal." He missed the old me, and I did not know where she had gone. At my lowest point, I thought about the world being better off without me, one of the most "woe-is-me" victim statements ever. What snapped me out of it were three very distinct thoughts all in rapid succession:

- I could never do that to my mother
- I could never do that to my children
- Mark would remarry within two years because he is such a nice guy

The vision of the endless parade of casseroles from neighbors and introducing Mark to their single friends snapped me out of my victimhood in under 30 seconds. That is when I realized how mad I was at him for not looking harder for a job and had not voiced it. After two long bouts of unemployment, I did not see him really trying to rectify the situation. For too long, I backed off because I did not want to hurt his feelings while ignoring my feelings and needs. It was literally eating me alive.

The air, the element of the heart chakra, came flooding back into my lungs and heart and out through my throat. It was harsh, and I spoke it in harsh tones. It was my truth. It felt almost like I was vomiting from swallowing so much toxicity. It may sound gross but throwing up can feel really good and is important when you have the flu.

At first, Mark was taken back and defensive, and we got pretty loud with each other. I finally asked him to stop telling me about only finding the jobs he didn't want and that he needed to get clear about what he did want. Was it money, a title, stock options? Without hesitating, he responded that he wanted to work for a company like the one he used to work for. One where employees actually know one another, and every person mattered. One where he could do minimum travel because he missed the kids so much when he was away. He wanted to be known by his first name, not the sales numbers he put up. He wanted to matter to his employer. And for that they would receive a dedicated employee.

Shortly after that outburst, just such a position opened up. Mark applied, and within two months of his outburst, he was happily employed. But first, we had to erupt. Together we liberated our separate truths of what did not work for us so we could be in right relation with our hearts and future employers.

In this example, you can see how once you look into your heart, it is important to then speak your truth which leads us to the throat chakra.

Throat Chakra: Open Authentic Communication

Color: Robin's egg blue. Element is Vibration/Sound. Location: Throat. In charge of Voice/Expression, Larynx, Thyroid, Parathyroid, Arms, Hands.

This chakra is where we speak truth. Not the truth but true-to-oneself kind of truth. It is tied directly to the sacral chakra in terms of creativity. If we want any of our creations to come to fruition or gain the ability to liberate an undesirable situation, we must express it. It is where we find our originality. Spoken, written, tapped out in Morse code. Expression and communication sit squarely in this chakra. It is also where we express our creativity. When not in alignment, we may experience laryngitis, vocal cord problems, a sore throat, a cough that lands in our throat, thyroid problems.

Hear Me Roar

My bouts of laryngitis were about to come to an end. The days of sore throats and constant frogs, those phlegm balls that clog the airway and repeatedly needed clearing were done. The doubling over waiting for external approval would go from a whimper of pain to the roar of a Leo, which I am not (but Mark is.) Heady with power, I released, I screamed, I demanded to be heard. I liberated all that was stuck in my root, sacral, solar plexus, and heart. I released all the thoughts, beliefs, and unshareable responsibility for where I was at in life. The work I once loved became a place I went to fulfill an overwhelming financial responsibility. This place was filled with

44

people I did not like and could not trust. The home I used to come back to and relied on became foreign and unrecognizable. The husband with the strong work ethic was working on everything except getting a new job. I felt unsuccessful, powerless, unappreciated. I just wasn't enjoying the life I had. I was learning what I needed and fiercely sharing it. Voiced in a way that no one could ignore. Not even me.

Just thinking about it all these years later still gives me a rush of power. Eventually, I would learn how to channel my voice for greater good but not at first. First it was just a tea kettle obnoxiously whistling, boiling over, screaming from the heat. So, I removed myself from the heat by doing the unexpected. I quit my job… And it was So. Damn. Freeing. And, because it was new and unexpected for me, Mark heard me. Not that I was a shrinking mouse. I have never been that. I have always freely expressed my opinions, and they were usually about what others should be doing or why I was right. However, this time, my truth did not include any reassurances that I could handle things and was without the woe-is-me. It was honestly the first time that I had said, "I can't handle it anymore." I replaced fault with truth. I unleashed the anger in all the right places, including at myself. The definition of depression – anger turned inward - came spewing forward in demonstration of all the unexpressed anger now being vehemently expressed. Who cares if the world would be better off without me? It would not be better off without me. I am here for a reason.

When my voice came forward, so did the squeaky ethereal sounds of orchestral instruments tuning up to play a melody. The sacral and the throat, the co-creators of joy and pleasure and truth, came together to help me in the messy stages of learning to play my own instrument. I remember the sounds coming from upstairs while my fifth grader took up her first violin, and my eighth grader practiced the viola in preparation for the school concert. The playful metaphor reminded me of how much things can improve over time, with a little practice. It was a reminder that this recognition and expression of truth was new to me and would take some practice before the sounds brought pleasure to anyone's ears.

There is a difference between talking, talking loudly, expressing opinions, and directly speaking your truth. It is an important distinction because there is no such thing as the truth, only my truth and your truth. My truth did not require anyone else to accept it, but I was obligated to express it if I wanted to be in right relationship with others and this world. It was equally important for me to learn to ask more questions to get beyond what others expressed and what was the guiding thought behind it. Was Mark saying, "no, I won't get a job" or was he saying, "I don't know what I want or how to find it?" Was Mark saying to me, "pull yourself together and get back to work?" Was he trying desperately to be supportive while taking on new concerns about our financial well-being? Was Mark acting aloof to distance? Was it a reflection of the distance he felt from me, or was he giving me the gift of space?

You know that funny thing of hearing yourself for the first time when the words leave your mouth? There was a lot of that going on. I could express how angry I was, how much I loved my family, how exhausted I was, how much I did not want to lose, how much I could no longer take on. There were surprises along the way, especially if I heard myself say something I did not mean or said it with an intent to harm. Wounding another does not help the situation. Squeaky, raw, honest, would eventually give way to more thoughtful and constructive and still honest exclamations. Self-soothing was also key. Forgiving myself would eventually lead to positive conversations with myself and others. But it was a progression. First, I had to expel all the crap that had built up inside of me. I needed a balanced approach to life.

My warning to others is this: if something isn't working for you, if it is taking your mental and physical health, do not wait until it is a perfectly formed thought before releasing it. Do not wait until you have the answer or diplomacy or grace. Get rid of it quickly so you can breathe and get really clear. You must get rid of the blockage before you can do anything else. I used to laugh at the notion of scream therapy sessions. Now I get it.

Third Eye Chakra: Intuitive Awareness

Color: Indigo. Element: Light. Perspective/Vision located in the center of the forehead. In charge of: Eyes and Sinuses

This chakra is like a zoom lens that can zoom out to expand and take both the bigger picture and the ability to zoom in on specific details. It is best used when swiveled both inward and outward.

Perspective tells you how you might want to apply energy in a clear way for maximum impact. When not in alignment, we may experience vision problems, migraines (also related to the solar plexus), sinus infections, blindness (literal or metaphorical), inability to see a way out.

Perception is Everything

In my years as a psychic and tarot reader, I have come to appreciate the Death card. So often confused for something horrible, it is simply saying that "a situation is coming to an end. Here is the opportunity to envision something new."

Clarity is a rare gift. It sometimes comes from concerted effort and other times in surprise bursts. At the time of my vocal eruption, it shook off or greatly loosened many of the specks that blinded this beautiful indigo energy disc. I could feel my fisheye lens of a third eye rapidly rotating from inside to outside, from narrow to wide focus, from self to others, from situation to situation. The light was flooding in. What a big ugly mess with a glorious view.

The old me wishes I could tell you that I did all this sorting by myself, but the new me accepted a new kind of help and a new kind of redirection of all victimhood statements back to myself. We have all experienced leaders who thought they had to have all the answers would not accept counsel. It can be painful to watch their inevitable self-destruction. None of what I am reporting here happened without the persistent help of a holistic practitioner and the incredible counselor who was willing to hold a safe space for me to explore despite much of this not being in her textbooks, at least not in this way. Painful, exhilarating, frustrating, empowering, imperfect. A big part of perspective is allowing input from others. Allowing input from other professionals was very clarifying. Saying I could not afford to spend the money right then would have had a devastating and limiting impact on the outcome. I realized I had to spend money on myself. From what I could discern in twelve years of Catholic schools, the only reward for martyrdom was early death. Perspective and education are hugely important to this process.

With the help of professionals, voraciously reading self-help books, and sustained meditations, this is where the power of thought came into focus for me. I could look at the same situation through various perspectives and it would look different with each glimpse. When I landed on a thought that was both loving and positive, I would consciously follow it.

For example, I could choose to see Mark's distancing as resisting what was happening for me or I could see him as giving me the space I needed. He researches everything and none of this amorphous blob was coming up in any search engine. Don't get me wrong, there was plenty he did resist and sometimes still does. He was unimpressed with my new spoon bending abilities, and that really hacked me off. But as time goes on, I am getting better at seeing his need to know something is for sure as his problem and allow him to grapple with the uncertainty. In the past, we insisted that one see things from the other's perspective. It turns out, it is not always necessary, nor does it mean you cannot come to a joint decision. What it does do is free me and him from needing the other one's approval of our process for how we come to our individual decisions.

Years ago, when I read the Celestine Prophecy, I was struck by the concept of the Four Control Dramas: interrogator, intimidator, woe-is-me, and aloof. We can call on any of them from time to time, but one will tend to be our primary default. To me, Mark is the interrogator, and as I already admitted, I am the woe-is-me. This early lesson came crashing back to me when I would learn to look for the motivation for the behavior separate from the behavior. I wanted to be rescued. Mark wanted to understand. His way of understanding was to have more details, more facts, which I did not need, and I felt bullied by his persistence. We both expressed our needs by getting louder but not necessarily clearer. As I worked to liberate whatever was not working, my insistence that he was bullying me and that I was a victim had to go.

As I gained this perspective on how I was reacting to things and took responsibility for it, it became easier to recognize his reaction not as a reflection of me but of how he responds to uncertainty in general. It gave new meaning to the ouch-y realization that no one can shame me without my permission, without giving away my personal power.

Crown Chakra: Spiritual Awakening

Color: Violet. Element: Ether. In charge of Openness to Source/Wisdom Located: Top of the head. In charge of Brain, Pituitary Gland, Cerebral Cortex, Central Nervous System

The crown chakra is our connection to the Sacred. It is where we surrender to the angels or Spirit or God or a higher power of one's choosing that which we wish to liberate from our life. We surrender to a more powerful guidance or greater clarity that things must change. Here is where we open to new thoughts, ideas, and ideal futures. We allow for guidance. When unbalanced, we can have delusions, dissociate, or suffer from incoherent thoughts. This is where our thoughts can haunt us and our dysfunctional stories grow in fear. It is where depression comes from.

Open Source Communication: Let Go and Allow

The final step in liberation is release. Release to the angels, Spirit, Universe, whatever you wish to call it. Just let it flow up into divine white light so you can see the good in all of it and let go of all else, especially any deranged thoughts that you might not be worthy. Keep the lesson. Lose the baggage. Sometimes a comeuppance is a good thing. I have come to appreciate that the lesson is in the sting. If something causes me to feel uncomfortable, that is where my next lesson lies. I felt the sting often when I enrolled in a course about white privilege. It wasn't because I was a bad person that the lessons hurt. It called out how mindlessly and matter of factly I walked through life believing my experience was within other people's realm of experience. It is not. I learned that two people walking into the same situation can and do experience it differently. I was not aware or awake, and my insensitive actions showed it. Those lessons came almost ten years after my breakdown. At that time in my life, the sting was in my victim's story and false belief that I could handle whatever life throws at me. Worse yet, was how often I accepted what was thrown at me without question. And that is the point, I needed to question everything until I found what was true for me and not assume it was true for anyone else.

The "sting" in this story is realizing that I relinquished my power to others, especially Mark. I expected him to see things from my perspective without having to point it out. I assumed he was having the same experience as me, and that was far from the truth. He was having his experience and I was not aware because I was equally wrapped up in mine. Mark needed me to encourage him to live into his strengths and for me to set more boundaries by clearly expressing how low my fuel tank was running. Instead, I chose martyrdom. When I was able to see that Mark's life was about him and not me, a lot of things became clearer. My life was my responsibility.

The crown chakra, the ether, is a two-way communicator. It is the energy of violet light, the least dense color of the chakras. When I reached this uppermost energy body, I was overwhelmed with love and acceptance. They -- Spirit, Angels, God, Universe -- had been waiting for me, patiently, ready to accept me as a flawed soul learning powerful lessons. Some might call this religion, but it was devoid of doctrine and dogma and tenets. It was an uncovering and a knowing beyond any human-made religion. This, I thought, is what some clergy fear: when followers find that powerful direct connection with God. Unfiltered, unabated, uncontrolled. Direct. Loving without exception. Devoid of heaven or hell. Just love and compassion and full of second chances. I rested here for quite a while letting the tears of joy and relief wash over me. If I hadn't known it before, I sure as heck knew it now. The Divine Being we often think of as God has no care for labels. Be it those of race, gender identify, sexual preference, religious affiliation, or vices. There is only our vibration and the need to understand what our vibration brings to the world. A Course in Miracles says there are only two emotions: fear and love. Fear is earthly and Love is in the upper reaches of our energetic being. All there is after this lifetime is love. For me, that is not a belief but a true knowing.

With this learning, I found the courage to liberate a whole lifestyle that wasn't working for me. I wish I could tell you that was the end of my journey, but it is just the beginning of this next leg, and it was a doozy. Even while surrounded by love from above, I now had to thoughtfully manifest my new reality with some stinging reminders yet to come. And because I had felt that unrelenting love and acceptance, I could no longer pretend I had a choice other than to explore and accept who I am. Perhaps the biggest piece was coming out of my closet of "otherness." Once I started communicating directly with the Divine, many other gifts, talents, and realizations came pouring in causing a constant need for consideration and chakra balancing. This is where I met my angels who gladly lifted my burdens; my guides who welcomed my confusion; my higher self that knew all along I could live my life with less angst. If God isn't judging me, then who am I to judge?

I once had a joke question in an essay: "Define the universe and give three examples." Of course, the joke is everyone "knows" there is only one Universe and it is all encompassing. Now I know the joke is on us. Now I am aware that there are many universes and we as humans cannot ever really know of everything that is existence. Seeing the meta worlds would overwhelm us and distract us from our work here in this lifetime. I cannot describe how I saw that my energetic vibration, my thoughts and whole being were separate from and completely interwoven to all of life, throughout the universes and galaxies and heavens. Powerful, uplifting, and devoid of all excuses. There was so much out there that one single universe could not contain it all and no language could adequately describe it. At this point, what I knew for certain, was that whoever I am and whatever this lifetime holds for me, it is a gift. That knowing was so powerful it became a commandment to embrace all of life, including the rough times and memorable lessons.

Exercise 3:

Revisit your earlier notes of a situation you feel is particularly stuck or otherwise not working for you. A situation you feel you cannot change no matter how hard you try.

1. Closing your eyes and taking a deep breath, bring your attention to your root chakra. See that situation in the red glowing disc at the base of your spine. Notice how it looks and feels.

2. Begin to move the situation up through each successive chakra, noting how it feels (sacral), how it may impair your personal power or ability to digest life (solar plexus), notice how easily you can or cannot breathe when you consider it (heart), speak your truth about how you feel about the situation (throat), ask for perspective on this situation in a bigger context (third eye), and then see yourself releasing it through the crown.

3. Repeat this exercise several times and notice what new thoughts pop up, even (or especially) if they are seemingly unrelated to your initial query.

Mary Flanagan Gleason

Part IV

MANIFESTING FROM THE TOP DOWN

As I reached the uppermost chakra, I was able to release whatever issue had presented itself. I could say with complete confidence that "I am done with this" and release it for transmutation. I am open to something new that will more fully serve me and my life's purpose. While liberating ends at the crown, it is also where manifesting begins.

Manifesting works its way down the energetic spinal column, through all the other chakras landing at the root where it becomes reality. As this happens, I encountered more unresolved flecks, a dreaded feeling of familiarity and frightening feelings of unfamiliarity. At every step, I wondered how this would play out with others in my life. I worried about what others will think and how I can make this comfortable for them. I can't. Not my job. Easy to say, tough to do. Yet, none of it let me off the hook for being true and compassionate in my sharing.

Another amazing thing happens: the more certain I became about myself, the more separate I became from others' motivations. I began to see others for who they are and how my reaction to them plays into a dynamic for better or worse. When the interrogator meets up with the woe-is-me, the latter has lost all control. To be completely contrary and bizarre, I saw my interconnectedness to others and found that I am never truly alone. This is not meant to be preachy. It just is. Enlightenment brings with it the double edge sword of freedom and responsibility.

After these first few direct interactions with the Divine and initial glimpses into the great expansiveness of all there is, it is easy to see how some might feel superior. Like an astronaut might feel having walked on the moon when so few others had or might ever. Like getting that next promotion or buying that bigger house. Feeling superior is a hindrance to sustained enlightenment. Humility is a must. It turns out for me, that discovery and sharing are a part of my life's purpose. I know now that I am the archetype of priestess/teacher. I endeavor to remain a fellow seeker exchanging experiences and realizations with those who care to do so, although I do not feel called to evangelize. If nothing else, I have learned that each soul finds their way in their own time and for their own reasons. My goal is to offer community and a sense of belonging, which I so deeply craved and found in so many curious places.

My first real challenge presented itself from the first time I sat in the silence, and the angels rushed in, and I do mean rushed! They were relieved to see me. It turns out that angels are always there for us, but they do not intervene without our expressed request or invitation to do so. Some call it prayer.

The first time I sat in silent meditation and began getting incredible messages, whole concepts without language, and overwhelming feelings of love, I could feel the tears flow down my cheeks, and I would smile. I felt lighter. Immediately I began hearing from passed loved ones I had never met but who were anxious to talk with other living relatives. In one of my earliest experiences, I saw my uncle and aunt, my mother's older siblings, both of whom died when my mother was young. My uncle was wearing his army uniform and swinging from a German Street sign. He died in WWII in the Black Forest of Germany. My aunt was in her wheelchair. Of all the things I could have asked, I asked why my aunt was still in a wheelchair and my uncle in his uniform. They answered without hesitation: "so you would recognize us." That made perfect sense since they were dressed exactly like in the photos my grandmother had kept on her dresser. As the tears streamed down my physical body, I felt an energetic embrace and melded into their soulful presence. They had come forward because they said my mother was worried that she was going to die. They wanted me to tell her that she was fine, but she did need to see a doctor. I told her the next day and she admitted she was sleeping sitting up in a chair because she began to choke every time she laid down. With this message of assurance, she finally went to the doctor who prescribed something for her reflux and explained ways to avoid it. The problem and the fear went away. I felt blessed to be the conduit to answer my mother's prayer.

This encounter made me realize how powerful I am, how easy it is, and how resisting that time of silence each day had meant missing out on so much love and guidance. It was also another step further away from who I had been. Sharing this with Mark was weird, and he had no way to calculate it, an untenable situation for someone with his engineering background. Still, that powerful Genie was out of the bottle, and I liked it. I finally felt right.

I also began to know things that had always been there, but I could not see, to feel a new level of both power and dread. In earlier years, I had flashes of parallel universes and lifetimes in my waking day. They remained tucked away in my memory, unshared with another. Like when I went to a crowded street festival and saw a farmer with his yoked oxen plowing the fields as if the crowd or even the town did not exist. No one else could see him and he could not see us, but he was there. I knew it was real, that somehow there was a hole in the veil of separation, but I kept it to myself. Another time I saw a man from about fifty or more years before (judging by his clothing) standing in what is now the middle of a major highway. He was enjoying the view, resting, unaware of any cars or roads. Maybe he was dead now, or maybe not. Maybe he was still alive and recalling a special moment. But again, a peek through the veil at a glimpse in time. Now, here I was seeing them in real time all at once, separate and together. How on earth was I going to tell anyone? For sure, my engineering, logic-driven, five-senses dominant husband was not going to get this. My mother was curious but unsure of how to think about it. I am guessing she did not share this with her friends when listing my accomplishments. My children would have new fuel to prove their mother was weirder than yours. But most of all, how was I going to embrace myself in new ways? How would I show myself compassion and a more thoughtful, less rushed way to each new decision? Decisions that would by necessity include information divined from above without proof.

There were far more questions than answers. And conversely, more answers than questions I had ever thought to ask. My curiosity fully engaged, I devoured books like those by Byron Katie, Jerry and Esther Hicks, Ekhart Tolle, Elizabeth Gilbert, and most anybody who had appeared with Oprah Winfrey with messages about intuition, spirituality, psychic abilities, mediumship, coming into their own truth. What was even scarier was how many books I found on my own bookshelf that I had picked up and maybe never read or read with less appreciation. I harkened back to some of my earliest encounters like Jonathan Livingston Seagull and *The Celestine Prophecy* and remembered so clearly that inkling of recognition. I ran to the theater to see What the Bleep Do We Know and cried with the realization that I was not alone. I had lived this way before and forgot. I had been guided with unseen information as a kid and as a young adult, and somewhere along the way, allowed it to be overruled or dismissed.

Before I recognized my intuitive abilities, I received many messages about current situations while asleep or standing in the shower or driving in the car and simply accepted them as an obvious truth. The more immersed I became in the data-driven world, the less I listened. Not consciously but just gradually slipped into a tangible, orderly, Muggle world. But not once did the angels stop talking. They are a patient and persistent lot.

So, when I was recovering from the emotional and physical trauma, I got really picky about what would come back into my life and what had to stay out. Let the enlightened manifesting begin from top to bottom. From thought to reality.

Crown Chakra: Recognize Your Divine Creative Power

The crown chakra is our connection to the Sacred. It is where we open to new thoughts, ideas, and ideal futures. We allow for Divine guidance. When in alignment, we receive ideas and concepts that inform our lives for the better. We accept that we are powerful spiritual beings having a human experience.

Satellite Dish at My Command

The crown chakra works like a satellite dish. It can be focused as desired. Am I ready for huge concepts, or do I need more specific input? I set the intention to open to information that is only for my greatest good and highest purpose. I would soon come to appreciate that my stomach ulcers were my unconscious choice because the Spirit starts with gentle energetic taps or attention getters and turns up the intensity until you can no longer ignore it. A bout of indigestion, a little reflux, a low simmering sensation, an outright burning, to outright fear of eating. Okay! You got my attention! It may have landed in my stomach, but it first came from challenging intuition and accepting my thoughts, even when they were not in my best interest.

One of the last full-time jobs I took was a doozy. I hated everything about it but told myself, "I can handle it." Why? Because it paid more than the job I had before. That's it. We needed the money. That is how I reasoned away what my intuition was trying so desperately hard to tell me. We need the money. Do it anyway. So many warning signs were ignored. If I am completely honest, I would have to say that the Universe had been trying to get my attention with more subtle ailments like migraines, prickly skin, dreams, and indigestion, long before then. With the ulcer diagnosis and my feelings of being tremendously overwhelmed, they now had my complete attention. Letting it get that far was my choice. At first, I felt like a new driver, starting out slow, unsure how to handle this piece of machinery that could easily double as a weapon. How will I steer this? How will I honor it? What is too fast? Too slow? And a whole lot of "Oh my! When did all this power, energy, and love arrive?"

Over time and many meditations, I picked one situation or person and held it up to the light, checking to see if any dark flecks needed cleansing before re-entering. Kind of like wiping your feet before entering the house. If I found flaws, it was cause for further calculations. Is it worth cleaning off? Is it worth allowing back in? What will happen if I don't? What would work better for me? Often, I found what was acceptable and what was not with each situation. I had a friend with bipolar issues who did not want any medications and thought that once everyone knew what her situation was, we simply needed to allow her to be mean, rude, moody, and we would all just walk on eggshells for her. For a long time, I thought so, too. "Oh, she can't help it." When I challenged that belief and its effect on my life, it was easy to see how this served her but not me. Done. Gone.

But not everything is all or nothing. I can let Mark back in and not be in charge of providing the myriad details he requires. Letting him back in is love. Allowing time for him to gather the details without accepting responsibility for another's needs is loving myself. More importantly, he gladly took responsibility for his own needs. This way of thinking became my new filter. The more conscious everyday choices felt, the more I felt in control. It became less about what happened to me and more about how much I would allow it to impact me. Leaving a job where meanness and backstabbing were the norms from the top down was more than a no brainer. It was essential to my health.

Of course, the children were a shoo-in. After all, they are here by my invitation. There is a level of responsibility associated with parenting that does not belong in other relationships. Children are newly forming humans. Here was my opportunity to demonstrate loving boundaries and thoughtful acceptance of others. Later, I realized that I still could decide how much energy I would give to each child and the importance of letting them find their own solutions. Just because you are my child does not mean all you do is acceptable nor my responsibility.

A new maxim became my motto: No effort on your part means no effort on mine. If we are to be friends, we give and take in equal measure. In marriage, I need a partner that is both give and take. We have an ongoing conversation about what it means to have Mark lean in more to my life, especially in light of how much I have tried to lean into his. It didn't take him long to see I had no eye-hand coordination and golf was not my sport. But I tried. He could see, too, that home brewing his own beer was very heavy on the math and chemistry side and I did not enjoy brewing although I did attend a few brew days with him and his buddies. So, it is with some level of expectation, that I would appreciate him leaning in a bit more to some of my world. Anything less misses the opportunity for greater understanding. However, I also have to come to respect what Mark can realistically give to me. He tolerates my pursuits, but he does not fully support them. I feel bad sometimes, but the truth is that Mark does not need to accept every aspect of me, and my insistence is only me once again giving away my power. I must respect how much he cares about me overall and accept that as love. As one person said, "Let him off the hook. He's still a good guy."

In a world organized and built by engineers, communicating with them would be easier if I could offer something tangible, with parameters rather than expansiveness. It would help if what I said "made sense" a law of the five physical senses. This is where, for me, that feeling of being outside of the community can kick in. This is also where I have learned to resist the urge to hide my intelligence. The five senses and the sixth sense are not a dichotomy but an additional way for all of us to consider new possibilities. I hold my head up, more certain than ever that intuition is a valued, and rare offering to the world.

I have learned to welcome in Spirit with its sometimes loud and sometimes gentle voice. I live open to those messages I had ignored earlier. The messages are not always clear, a little pet peeve I have with Spirit, but that is my challenge. Metaphor, a favorite language of Spirit, is only so clever, and then I prefer full sentences. Still, it is always what I need to hear.

Thus, begins my manifesting in the violet flame of the crown. In addition to the rushing in of Spirit and angels and passed loved ones, I found a purity of truth that arrived without judgment or insistence. It was mine to embrace or ignore. That truth was that I was more powerful living into my intuition than I was trying to live into conventional ideas of success. When I accepted these messages as

Divine guidance, I could sense my ability to succeed greatly improve on every level. Still, that left the task of answering some tough questions.

- What exactly does it mean to live into being intuitive?
- How am I going to pay the bills?
- How will I tell Mark?

Spirit cared about none of these questions. That was my job. Spirit's job was only to present information and insights in the highest order of light and love. There is a very physical feeling to all of this and most especially in the crown chakra. It can envelop one's whole being and make you know to your very core that you are love, loved, and powerful in very scary ways. This helps when examining one's thoughts. Those with lower vibrations are instantly recognizable by their heft and dull sound, like a rock passing through feathers. Committing to a job I did not want, agreeing to a task I am not committed to, pushing aside my own well-being in favor of another are all things that land swiftly and heavily and throw me off balance. When thoughts like this land in my gut, it is clear that it is no feather. With each meditation, the vibration was so pure and honest that it made it impossible to ignore it.

My resolve to live into this new way of being was reaffirmed every time I engaged. To find a way to make it work, I had to be very careful and thoughtful of what I truly want to say, how I truly want to show up. That blamey, whiny thing turns people off and is part of my old playbook. But it would take lots of time and continued practice to make that mind shift to where my communications started with me. Like the "I-statements-only rule" in facilitated meetings. More than at any other time, I became aware of the power of my thoughts both mental and spoken. It scared and exhilarated me. Still does.

Now I tell you all of this awakening business as if it were a quick and obvious process but all of what I have described so far came in uneven bursts over several years and continues to reveal itself now and forever. Sometimes, sitting in the silence is just that. Silence. The messages come when I most need them and am open to hearing. Each "aha" running from top to bottom for consideration. Next stop: Can I see how this might fit with my new life?

Third Eye Chakra: Create a Vision

The third eye has a zoom lens that can expand to take in more information and focus on specific details. It is best used when deployed both inward and outward. Perspective helps you determine how you wish to apply energy for maximum impact. When in alignment, it is easier to trust our path and take advantage of things we see along the way.

Vision

With each new thought, concept, idea, I needed perspective.

- How might this show up in my life?

- Where does it fit?
- Where am I holding judgment about it?
- Is it true?

Like a fisheye lens, I had to turn the third eye both inward and out. Sometimes I saw what was before me, and other times I saw what the future might look like in each circumstance. Always, I felt the energy and power of thought.

I noticed if a thought felt light or heavy, was dynamic or static. Sometimes, a thought had color which gave me clues to understand where this would be reflected in my chakras. For example, am I holding on to something in my gut (yellow) or heart (green)? I allowed each thought to play out as if in a dream and then mentally bring in other people and situations to see how they might interact. This can happen quickly, or it can take a long time in one or more meditations. Sometimes perspective came in dreams. There are times when my third eye simply tingles, or I feel the need to scratch my brow; just another sign to pay attention, get perspective, get clearer.

As I questioned what this intuitive knowing meant for my life moving forward, I got the clear message that I would heal and help others heal as well, yet medicine was not my thing. That led me to wonder what it would mean for me to be a part of another's healing journey.

Eventually, I came to realize that healing would mean channeling messages from Spirit in psychic readings or connecting people with their passed loved ones and helping them re-examine the stories that held them back with false beliefs. Better still, I would come to help others connect with their intuition and begin to nurture their awakening.

I've never gotten the hang of reading auras, the colorful energies that emanate from one's physical being. Still, I recognized that I could sense and gain information if I simply allowed my mind to engage another's chakras. In one of my earliest experiences, I simply closed my eyes and imagined I was the woman before me. As I mentally scanned her body, I noticed where the energy felt stuck or even had twinges of pain. I asked if she experienced a lot of lower back pain. Yes, she did. Then I asked her if she was more worried about having children (sacral chakra = creation) or money (root chakra = safety.) Both, she said. Then with her eyes still closed, I asked Spirit for some specific guidance and was shown a knight on a white steed whisking her away. She was not resisting, nor was she not smiling. It was more a resignation on her part. She was focused on being rescued. In this way, her happiness would be in another person's hands. When I shared this with her, the tears flowed. She said she never really did want children or to be married, but now, in her late thirties, she wondered if that would be a better choice since she did not want to work anymore. She worried about saving for retirement and who would take care of her in her old age. In her mind, a husband would somehow naturally come with a 401K, and raising children would be about what she needed long term, not the desire to grow souls. She recognized that her newly developed desire for a husband and children were more fear-based and wanting to avoid specific decisions she needed to make. Once we had this vision clarified, Spirit went on to deliver other messages. I would come to learn that connecting with others' chakras is a big part of my zone of genius, and the healing effects would grow to become more and more apparent. I was able to help my client rephrase the question to ask Spirit how she might be most successful moving forward. Spirit answered that question in a way that made her feel lighter, truer to herself, and more in control of her future.

I also began to envision my new future beyond the next year or two. What was my future without the old precepts, and how would I begin to manifest it? The one I like to toy with the most is where the money will come from. Spirit laughs, only reassuring that it flows to me easily and often. I added it to my list of affirmations and moved on. I learned to pick up pennies on the ground, enjoy a surprise discount at the checkout, and an airline voucher for overfull flights as evidence that money does indeed flow to me. It pays to be open and to recognize abundance in all its many forms. Mark agrees with this in general, but like many people, a penny on the ground represents one cent rather than abundance. That begs the question of what is enough?

What does a sign of prosperity and abundance look like to you? What signs might you be ignoring? What I have learned so far is that signs of abundance are everywhere if I look for them. Remembering that we find what we seek, I choose to seek abundance. I pick up the penny.

On a more practical note, I learned to pay attention to those flashes that come in the middle of the day, seemingly out of the blue. For example, not that long ago, I got into my car in the dark with my protein shake and water bottle to head to the 5:30 am spin class. As I placed the protein shake in the drink holder, I had an instant vision of a deer in the road about a mile and a half from my house. It was very foggy that morning, but there was no fog in my vision. It was so real to me that I took that extra second to tell myself to remain vigilant lest a deer jump out in front of me. Lo and behold, at the exact spot I envisioned, the fog was gone, and there was a doe standing smack in the middle of the road! I was so grateful that I had the presence of mind to honor this vision. The doe gave a very nonplussed glance and slowly walked away. Not every vision is a grand event, but they are all informative.

I tell all of my clients about the importance of vision in leading your life or your organization. You need to have that big goal that is just out of reach that keeps you focused and so you know how best to allocate resources. A plan without a vision is a wish list. A plan with a vision is a priority list. For my life, I envisioned myself before audiences of all sizes. I am talking about spirituality and self-awareness as healing tools by first healing one's thoughts to lead a more fulfilling life. Eventually, I would come to present workshops and talk with small groups. But first I had to envision it. Now, I see myself doing more presenting to audiences of increasing sizes and as part of panels of presenters whose work I admire. When I see this, I take time to imagine stepping into my future self and walk around in her as if it were true now. It is critical for successful manifesting to know what success feels like so I am can recognize it when it is happening.

For me, it feels like free-flowing air with a strong sense of belonging. Like I am in the right place. No imposter syndrome nagging at me. I belong in this group of thought leaders and healers. What I bring to the conversation is a welcome addition. I hold on to that vision and feeling so I recognize when I am closer or drifting away from it. Most importantly, I attract all the right people for whom my words and experience bring meaning to their lives.

I rehearse my interview with Brene Brown at least twice a week.

Throat Chakra: Communicate Your Vision

This chakra is where we speak our truth. It is tied directly to the sacral chakra in terms of creativity because for any of our creations to come to fruition, we must express it. As I said earlier, spoken, written, tapped out in Morse code, expression and communication sit squarely in this chakra. When in alignment, our voice is strong and confident, and our vision is clearly expressed.

Giving Voice to Ideas

Sound is quite powerful. Drums beating in tandem, orchestra strings plucking at our hearts, arias that take us on a journey of pain and loss even when we don't understand the words. Sound is powerful, and it is critical to our ability to manifest. Voice can take many forms including spoken language, written word, concentrated thought, music. Once you give voice to something you wish to manifest, stand back because it is on its way to you. The hard part is keeping track of your thoughts because you do not have to be intentional to manifest. Your thoughts, your snarky comments, your less than optimistic outlook are all it takes, and presto!... that will be on your path. Keep in mind that the Universe hears only positives. "I don't want to get sick" becomes "I want to get sick." The solution is to focus on the positive like "thank you for my continued good health." Staying positive in our thoughts and words is one of those practices that is lifelong. We must be ever vigilant to manifest only what we truly want. While it is good to be specific, be specific about how you want something to make you feel so the Universe is open to bring it to you in many ways, and so you'll recognize it when it arrives. If you want a home where you feel safe and can raise children that is great. Think that. If you want a home that is red with a white picket fence, approximately a half-acre lot within walking distance to the elementary school, it gets harder to meet the first two criteria. It's still possible, but it is good to know your most important criteria.

Beginning to recognize the power of voice, I gave resonance to my new and rediscovered abilities and I invited all opportunities to explore them further. This is called positive manifestation. For my career, I asked for a path that would respect what I had to offer and would no longer require me to work for one more intelligent yet deeply insecure boss. As I began to restart my consulting practice, I received a call from my minister who told me he took the liberty of throwing my hat in the ring with the stewardship consulting group of our faith tradition, the Unitarian Universalist Association. Here I found a community of stewardship consultants who I could call on for my work with congregations and other consulting clients, the opportunity to travel and meet other like-minded people, and to share my knowledge with people who welcomed it. I could not have asked for better. I was so beautifully aware that my clarity of thought and prayer brought about this opportunity: its resonance rang true on every level. Another community entered my life.

Mark and I had a funny exchange about manifesting one time. It was the week before Christmas, and we had to go to the mall. On a pleasant July day, the thought of going to the mall can send Mark into orbit, much less holiday time. However, this time the mall is where he could find this one item to complete the shopping for his family. On the way there, he screamed and fussed and used a lot of profanity about the certain lack of parking, that they were going to overcharge for the item, and he would no doubt have to wait in a long line to get any service. There was a time I would have engaged him, and we would have argued. I decided to try a different tactic. About two blocks from the mall, I challenged him to try it my way. I suggested that he thank the angels for a great parking spot, for finding the item he wanted easily and within budget, and for the ability to pay for it without waiting in line. In his typical east coast style, he sarcastically shouts in a mocking, nasally voice, "Thank you for the fucking parking spot, not raping me on the price and for bored salesclerks who skip wishing me a nice day." As we pulled into the very full parking lot, the car next to the entrance pulled out. "That was just coincidence," he proclaimed. "No such thing," I responded. As we walked into the store, there on the table by the door was the item he wanted for $39, a dollar under his $40 limit. Another coincidence? As he gruffly grabbed it like someone might take it from him or it would magically disappear when he woke from this dream, a very young salesclerk with slight shoulders and an oversized Adam's apple asked if he needed anything else. "No? I can ring you up right here." When we got back to the car, I finally asked if he thought there was anything to that manifestation stuff. He avoided all recognition but did not outright say no. It became a game for the rest of our outing, needing to stop at two more stores: each time, parking, price, and service all on demand. He changed the subject. I smiled.

When I was a kid, my mom and I flew to New York City to see the Thanksgiving Day parade in person. My father and brothers celebrated with my grandmother. It was just mom and me. As if that wasn't already the coolest thing ever, it was beyond cool to see those enormous balloon floats. Up close, we were in awe of the incredible amount of training and teamwork it took to manage them. Each balloon float had a team at street level, and each team member had charge of a rope hanging from various points on the underbelly of the float. The team knew how to keep Bullwinkle flying high without hitting buildings, taking down streetlights, and always smiling. The lead person had a special tee shirt that read "Macy's Balloon Captain." My mom and I pretended to be balloon captains for the rest of the day. I decided right then and there that was my career goal. Fast forward, I realize now how many times that is precisely the role I played in far too many jobs. I led teams through some crazy superimposed visions and down some narrow passageways, but we did it. Over the last fifteen years I have come to realize that I was really meant to be Bullwinkle, Winnie the Pooh, or some other magical character. I would be soaring at high heights and looking forward, taking in and sharing the higher view knowing that my team below would neither cut me loose nor steer me toward catastrophe. Mark mostly acts as my balloon captain now. I will have to get him a really nice tee shirt.

Perhaps my most significant request for positive manifestation was to step into who I am, no holds. Go big or go home, right? Several years into all of this, a neighbor invited me to join a business coaching group that began with the Myers Briggs Type Indicator. It was there that I came to appreciate what it actually means to be intuitive, how misunderstood intuition is (even by its owner), the many ways people put it to use, why people might fear it, and so much more. The group's motto was to "be unapologetically who you are." The opportunities presented in answers to my requests do not always flow on my schedule, but they always appear at exactly the right time. First, I had to give voice to what I wished to manifest. No magic wands. Directed energy and divine timing. And lots of patience, persistence and faith.

The group was full of dominantly intuitive people versus the five senses, and almost all women (one guy out of thirty-five members. Brave soul.) Still, it was hard for me to let down my guard and be seen as less than having it all together. The old training still deeply ingrained, still holding me back. It was the other group members who gently but firmly kept nudging me to get real. It was not enough for me to think or envision my future. I absolutely had to own my intuition OUT LOUD. Even though I had made a lot of progress, there was more for me to reveal to others with confidence. Sixty years of conditioning to "never let them see you sweat" and conventional definitions of acceptability may have had something to do with it, but it was time for me to get out of that mindset. Again, I was being challenged to get out of my own way. Turns out, the weirder I got, the greater the acceptance. It was not someone else's definition of weird that was holding me back. It was my own special form of self-limiting beliefs. It took two long years to go from weird to authentic. So worth every damn minute. How could I ask others to accept the new me if I could not speak it confidently? I couldn't. As always, it was me that had to take the first step.

How we speak our truth matters. I had to recognize that my truth is only mine. Mark's truth was also true, even if it contradicted mine. I had to speak my truth with kindness and respect. I had to listen to Mark's truth with kindness and respect. Demanding another see things my way might work in the short run, but it is often short-lived. Again, another developing and imperfect practice. The more I gave thoughtful voice to my truth, the more thoughtfully Mark and others shared their truth. Less fighting, more understanding. More truth telling.

I would be remiss if I did not add that one very frustrating element of communication, is when receiving huge concepts that have no language. Engineers have the language of mathematics. Musicians have musical notes. Many of the messages I receive have no language. I have learned to say, "I cannot adequately describe what I know to be true. Bear with me."

Heart Chakra: Nurture Vision within Self and Others

This chakra resides at our core. When in alignment, it allows blood to flow throughout the body, and it is easy for us to breathe. It is how we are in relationship with other people and situations. It connects the lower three chakras to the three upper chakras.

Living in Right Relation

For every idea, request, and empowered vision for the future, I had to check in with my heart. I had to be honest with myself about how I felt about life with all these new twists and turns.

- How important are they if someone like Mark or others in my life do not accept it?
- Will I stay true to this newfound sense of self, or will I try to squelch it again?
- Am I in right relation first and foremost with myself and anything new I wish to manifest?

If an idea or way of being is born of revenge or victimhood, then it might feel good for a while, but its long-term effects will only set me back. If I come from a position of self-love and complete acceptance of self, then it is likely to move me forward. My test is in the ease of my breath and gentle or excited beat of my heart. That sensation we all sometimes get of a little man or even an elephant sitting on our chest signifies that something is out of right relationship. Something that is not for your greatest good. When I get in tune with those signals, I have learned to address it while it is a little man and not wait for it to grow to a full-size elephant. Too often, I would take something for the anxiety and continue to push on. It is far easier to deal with the symptoms than the cause. My stomach ulcers were a symptom and that is all traditional Western medicine tried to address. The cause of my pain manifested in ulcers, but no doctor wanted to talk about lifestyle and self-defeating behaviors. They did not see it as my personal power draining through a sieve which, of course, it was. So, paying attention to taking the right job for the right reasons is likely to show up here, in the heart, where breath and circulation and connection to others lie.

The question now becomes:

- Am I in right relation with this thought or idea?
- Is it first and foremost true for me?
- Is it born out of love for myself? Or my true passion?
- Does it propel me forward?

Then I must ask about my motives and what is the kindest and most effective way to share this with others who are important to me. Are they truly the people I want to be in relationship with? Answers to any of these questions can change at any time, so I must keep asking them and deciding how they make me feel.

- Is it a true and equal relationship of give and take? Not tit for tat, but I'll be there for you and you'll be there for me?
- Is this relationship or situation rewarding?
- How is this person or situation encouraging me to be better? Or is it?

Our marriage has been a bit of a slinky relationship. In my own Bullwinkle way, I tend to get way out ahead of Mark, and eventually, he catches up after he has gathered and studied all the data. Just when he's arrived, I have spied the next destination and jumped ahead once again. I soar from the third eye perspective, and he is a street-level balloon captain, one foot in front of the other. I am in the traffic helicopter, and he is the frustrated driver working the relentlessly slow-moving traffic on I-5, quite often cussing at the traffic reporter above. I can take it, though. I know that together we are going to get where we need to go. He needs to know that there is more in front of him than another person's tail pipe so we're good in that way.

Mark's lower chakra preference and my upper chakra approach to life meet right here, in the heart. We reconcile and support and balance each other. It is where intuitives and engineers meet. One sees, one does. One envisions, one builds.

Consulting the heart also helps me to choose friends more wisely. It even helps me choose causes that engage my passion and willingness to give away my precious resources. To know what is true and in alignment with my values, my greatest good, and the difference I wish to make in the world.

Heart dis-ease can indicate many things, including emotional heartbreak, a life lived out of alignment with one's self, maybe even martyrdom. It harbors unmet expectations of self and others if you let it.

Smoking takes our breath away. Yes, it is addicting, but it is also possible to stop. It must serve you better not to smoke than it does to continue to do so. But we do not stop until we are ready to reclaim our heart and breathe new life into it. Emotions like grief can clog our arteries. Unrelenting stress constricts our lungs. Unmet expectations break our hearts. Ignoring our personal power in deference to others can break our spirit. "After all I've done for you…" It is hard to break habits like smoking and staying in bad relationships, but as I said, it is possible and necessary if we are to live in alignment and authenticity. If your heart does not belong first and foremost to you, you just might be a candidate for a dis-eased heart.

Solar Plexus: Plan and Take Action

The Solar Plexus is all about personal power, living our truth and not letting others' opinions dictate what we know to be true for us. When in alignment, we set and observe healthy boundaries for ourselves. When strong, we are better able to digest life.

Feeling Energized

The next series of considerations includes:

- How empowered does this idea, concept, or thought make me feel?
- Is this just for fun, or am I really going to commit to this?

Discovering my intuitive abilities had to be more than a neat parlor trick or occasional experience. It became a commitment to consistently show up exactly as I am regardless of how others may perceive me.

When I think of those earliest days of consciously checking in, I can still feel the expansive energy that adds to the flow of air, clears my throat, easily gives way to new visions and opens itself to the angels. There is validation up and down the chakras, the spine, the central nervous system, the core of my being.

None of this was easy for my husband to get. What happens to all the hard data when you insist on running everything through these invisible energy bodies? Living in a high-tech corridor, my husband was not the only engineer in my life that either sidestepped the conversation or pretended not to notice. Many people would have felt more comfortable if I could only draw it out on a cocktail napkin.

At the beginning of my career as a fundraiser for nonprofits, I ran a very detailed, segmented direct mail campaign for a medical school, nursing school, and teaching hospital. I became a whiz at memorizing minutia such as zip codes, middle initials, and alumni graduation years. Setting up detailed alumni events and travel schedules was fun and interesting, and I was darn good at it. I especially loved traveling to different cities and relished finding my way around a new place. There was no handy access to GPS in those days and reading a map was trickier than one might think. There was a certain thrill at figuring things out, a grand sense of accomplishment. As my career took off, the further away I got from the details. My career was on a straight trajectory upward with lots of rewards. I loved meeting with donors and finding that connection between their philanthropic goals and those of the organization's. Over time and with more promotions, I found myself increasingly chained to my desk again, managing others, attending endless meetings, and always focused on budgets. I also suffered from migraines.

Later I would read in Louise Hay's *Heal Your Body: The Mental Causes of Physical Illness and Metaphysical Ways to Overcome Them*; that migraines are resistance to being driven. It hit like a punch to the gut, the chakra of personal power. It catapulted me to that next level of self-realization. All my life, I had just assumed you got a job, did the work, did it better than anyone else, and continually received promotions. And yet, here I was resisting it.

The thought that just because I can do something did not mean I should do it, even If it was new and interested me greatly. Migraines left me blinded, unable to see, to put one foot in front of the other. I remember telling Mark that a migraine was when a neighbor from three houses away sneezes and you take it personally. The pain is that sensitive. Now when I feel a migraine coming on, I lean into it by asking what is causing it. Is it something I can avoid or put off for a while? They have not stopped entirely, but they do carry new information for me. I have also gotten better at finding the triggers and work to avoid them.

At the time, though the thought there was another way for me to live more fully into who I really am did not yet exist in my mind, I only knew I was not successful being who I was. If truth be told, I am way better with "ish" than with details. Part of my success with more prominent roles was my ability to see patterns, be strategic, and motivate others. My sweet spot was donor connections. But when details would land back on my desk, I would crumble. I can put together a very detailed budget, but please don't ask me to be an accountant or even a bookkeeper.

One thing that remained true and later became a sign of my intuition was my ability to go straight to the core of what someone was saying. Years later, when I told a group of former coworkers that I thought I might be psychic – a major personal revelation that I was entrusting them with - they gave a collective laugh. This was their response: "Duh!"

In Blink, Malcolm Gladwell cites research around intuition as "thin-slicing." Thin-slicing is one's ability to cut through all the incoming data and find the most critical element to focus on. In meetings, I tended to do just that. We would sit around the conference table hashing out problems and solutions, and I would often say, "Oh, you mean X," with X being what was at the heart of the matter. Sometimes it was received as brilliant and other times annoying or crass. It was not always appreciated. For some, the process of elimination or discernment takes longer. I may have even stolen another's joy of discovery in my direct route to the heart of matter. Now when I pick up signals from people around me, I try to be mindful to wait until I am asked for input or find a less direct path to speaking out. Somehow people do not like that creepy feeling that you are seeing them separate from their words. It is a valued trait for consultants and not so much for coaches, both of which I would go on to become.

Manifesting through the solar plexus requires thoughtful consideration of the pieces that matter, getting to the core of the issue, and honestly assessing what works for me. I would be remiss if I failed to mention ego. Ego lives squarely in the solar plexus. For me, it is the part that responds well to flattery (words of affirmation) and the belief that I can handle anything. Chakra balancing and manifesting require me to slowly and consciously discern opportunities that are good and those that are good for me. To discern between ego and Spirit is not as hard as one might think. Ego wants to have a conversation with you, keep you safe, keep you small, or even puff you up way outside of your capabilities. Spirit does not want to converse. Spirit's messages are quick, positive, and do not contract or exaggerate. Ego might say, "go ahead and see what happens. They might laugh. You might make a mistake." Or even, "go ahead and talk over others so they will think you know what you're talking about even if you don't. Never let them see you sweat." Spirit could be anything from "Yes," or "Keep looking" or "RUN!" Positive. Short. Without judgment. All for your greatest good and highest purpose.

The Sacral Chakra: Enjoy the Journey

The Sacral Chakra, with its water element oversees the flow of softening the earth and tempering the fire in the solar plexus just above. The sacral chakra is directly aligned with creativity and pleasure and emotions. When in alignment, you can derive pleasure from your life and feel like you are literally in the flow.

Finding Pleasure and Joy

The next step is to Marie Kondo the idea I'm considering. Does this bring me joy? Long term or short term? Is it just fun for now, or is it rewarding for some time to come? Both are okay, but if it is a really big idea then I want to again feel the expansive energy that gets swept up in the easy flow of creation. This chakra works with the throat chakra to create, giving the resonance and flow required for manifesting.

On the way down, I found the mess of furniture and murky waters had now organized itself. Mr. Conductor was poised at his stand, waiting for my nod to cue the orchestra; a silly visualization, but it worked for me. The most frustrating thing is that Spirit/Universe/Angels rarely talk in full sentences. They mostly work in metaphor, at least for me. The beauty and responsibility now open to interpretation. That is my job. It is your job, too.

- What am I going to do with this big idea, concept?
- Does it block my flow or easily sail along with it?
- Is it an effort to please someone else, or is it really what I want to do?

Once I do that, I am ready for the next step which includes really sitting with Mark to ensure he grasps the importance of what I am manifesting and finding where things are and are not negotiable. Every step is thoughtful and full of risk.

This is when I knew I could not return to the same work environment. The very thought of returning to consulting made everything feel better, in the flow. It was no longer a matter of Mark's approval and meeting household budgets but recognizing that if I stayed true to what I wanted to do, the money would follow as will all the other elements for a happier life. A few times I put my toe back in the waters of full-time employment, but it simply was not right. When you are on staff, people expect you to stay in your narrow lane, regardless of the connections you can see and draw to make things better. One of the perks of intuition is seeing the bigger picture, recognizing patterns, and making connections. My gift is in seeing how problems are forming and can be resolved or prevented altogether. I am not claiming that I was always right, but I was usually on to something important, not staying in my lane.

With equal fervor, I knew that I was also a gifted psychic and that whatever role I played as a professional or household contributor, that would take increasing prominence. Consulting is my zone of excellence. Intuitive work is my zone of genius, and I aim to live more fully into that. This is when the very thought of taking more classes, holding workshops, and inviting more learning opportunities into my life began to take hold and manifest. I especially love working with executives to understand and call on their intuition, to honor both the data stored in the left brain and the intuition and creativity in the right brain. I think of it as learning how to bring their whole brain to work.

It is deeply pleasurable and satisfying to help others feel empowered and to heal from limiting beliefs. The joy of people's gratitude is more than ego. It is validation that what brings me joy brings healing to others.

Part of the Myers Briggs Type Indicator describes being dominantly intuitive as being creative. This stumped me at first because I have never considered myself to be particularly creative. Now I know that my definition was simply too narrow. I created a grand vision for my life, a supportive community that is continually growing, and recognized and lived into a whole new way of being. Creativity is a survival skill that turns lemons into lemonade.

The Root Chakra: Ground Your Vision into Manifestation
When in alignment, we feel like we are standing on solid footing. We are happy or happier with what is in our lives. Things are manageable

and bring us a sense of balance. We feel like we have a leg to stand on.

Ask and Ye Shall Receive

Having filtered and considered my new sense of self, I knew I had no choice but to allow it to manifest in my life. I had to say, "I am psychic. I talk to dead people. I know things I cannot explain, and I trust them as my truth." That takes courage and determination. And it was just the beginning. The rest is my story of how that impacted me along the way, most especially married to an engineer who continues to ask, "WTF?"

Communication matters. Sometimes we receive information through feelings more so than words. My attempts to circumvent the criticism by acknowledging that "I know I'm weird" only served to sabotage my developing beliefs and sense of self. It is better to let other people form their own opinions. A fun thing that happens when I unabashedly say "I am psychic" is the number of people who are excited by it and want to discuss what that means and tell me all their experiences with the paranormal.

Not all dominant intuitives wish to hang out a shingle as a psychic. Some intuitives rely on their inner wisdom to incorporate this information without comment in whatever they are doing. This is especially true of successful CEO's and inventors. Jeff Bezos, the founder of Amazon, heavily relies on his intuition, as did Steve Jobs, co-founder of Apple, as does Arianna Huffington of the Huffington Post. They all value intuition as a partner in decision making. I love that so many intuitives can bring their whole brain to work. My mother and my grandmother did not think of themselves as intuitive or psychic. They called it "people sense," and they could spot a person's attitude and intentions upon walking in the door. For them, intuition was a big part of their survival kit.

I know a woman, "Toni" who is an especially gifted intuitive. In fact, she is so aware of her life's purpose that she uses her inner wisdom to propel her toward her goals. She knows that this is her last lifetime on earth and came to finalize some of the more social aspects of the soul. She told me about feeling blocked and somehow moving seemed like the way to get unblocked. So, she started looking at condos. Toni found one she wanted and made an offer. It was for more money than she would have gotten if she should sell her current condo. She was devastated to learn that the sellers did not want to accept a contingent offer. Toni was then motivated to put her condo on the market, and it sold in three days! There were three other units for sale in the same building that had been languishing for months, so she felt especially lucky. Now she realized she could buy the other condo. But this loud voice in her head kept telling her, "Do not buy." Why, she wondered. First Spirit encourages me to sell and now I'm hearing not to buy." She decided to rent for a year and reconsider her options. The sale of her condo closed at the end of July. Less than two months later, in September 2008, the economy crashed. All the equity from holding her condo for sixteen years was now cash in the bank and she purchased a new condo the following year at a much lower price.

Toni trusts her intuition over all other data or opinion. She knows that her intuition is there for her greatest good and highest purpose and abides by it above all else. Of course, it does not hurt that she was single at the time. If I had the same insights, I would have had no luck convincing Mark to move for no "apparent" reason.

As a young 20 something new in my career, I joked that having a sugar daddy would be nice. Then I met one, and it repulsed me. I knew then that I would not value what I did not earn. This whole enlightenment process spoke to how I wanted to manifest my life as much as what I wanted to manifest. Come as it may, I wanted to earn it. I continued working with a new appreciation for my own values and work ethic. Now I apply that ethic to hearing and trusting that inner knowing the way Toni does. When I do that, I attract the things that support me in my unapologetic way of living.

Having completed this process of liberating and manifesting many times. I can tell you that it has led me to greater focus, clarity of purpose, and a sense of peace at the root of everything I do. I continue to use this process on a frequent basis. Take just one thing that is niggling at me and run it up through the chakras and back down again until it is more clearly understood or even resolved. Among other things, I have manifested greater understanding of what it means to be intuitive; what it means to others who are more dependent on the five senses; writing this book; envisioning a whole new world and a way of being. And all of this in my sixties because it is never too late to grow and change. In this case, change means having more fully embraced who I have been all along.

A Few More Thoughts

Here is one grounding "aha" that came into my head: I came here at this time and with these people for a purpose. Working with past lives, both my own and others, I understood that we do not move on to the next lesson until we have learned the current lesson. I became determined to learn the lessons I chose for this lifetime now because I do not want to have to learn this lesson again. Coming into awareness of what does and does not work for me was a scary, empowering, and at times a reckless process. It felt disjointed, overwhelming, relieving, and reassuring, sometimes all at the same time. There was no priority order. The insights came in whatever order they came. Each came with "aha's" big and small, with fear and glee, with dream and relief, with release and responsibility. The hardest part is staying with it, staying true to the process, trusting the chakras and my guides who would help me accept responsibility for being my own savior. I had to openly and without reservation, embrace change in every area of my life.

Thinking about what others might think or judge was very hard to let go of. Hearing how I sounded outside of myself was horrifying. I was needy and victim-y. Equally hard to take was that I could no longer go on with the same success model. As I have said, the chakras had an organizing effect on the chaos, and they revealed my real self to me, warts, gifts, and all. The process revealed the gifts that are always a part of any situation. There is not one skill I learned that does not continue to serve me. I cannot stress enough that I did not do this work by myself. I had teachers and health care providers and family. I have new communities emerging one soul at a time.

Fortunately, I also had a husband that hung in there. It is not that Mark stood patiently back so as not to let his halo slip. There were many tough conversations, often loud. This was not a time for me to go off to one side and to go through a Kafka-esque experience while everyone else is pretending not to notice. I was going through a metamorphosis that impacted everyone around me, and I had to stay true to what I was becoming even when I did not know what that was. I prayed our marriage would remain intact, but I prepared to go if necessary because I would not ever leak that much personal power again. Being true to oneself, being selfish, is about as loving as it gets. Not the kind of selfish that gathers material things sometimes at the expense of others' very real needs, but in that deep knowing way that if I don't do this now, then I am a lie and so too is everything else in my life. The truth of me would have to be enough to build on.

Many police officers are intuitive, although stating that aloud or in those words might get them unwanted ribbing. Yet, many talk about their instincts or their gut reactions. Same thing. I sometimes think of police forces around the country attracting far fewer intuitive types when they switched from community policing models to more military structures. Military policing by its very nature is defensive. The military approach looks for possible threats and acts to eliminate them. It is based on the false reality of us versus them. We find what we seek. With community policing, officers are trained to get to know individuals on their beat, become a part of the community you serve. Act as a resource. Learn who is a possible threat and who has gone off their meds again? Who is new to the neighborhood and worthy of closer attention? Who can you trust to be straight with you? Less defensive posturing. More leaning in. Neither approach is without its issues but I'm not here to debate that. My point is more that we find what we seek. I write this as the sister of two retired police officers: one a successful beat cop, the other a successful detective known for his ability to solve cold cases. The first will tell you he is not intuitive, the second will tell you he is. I will tell you they both are. Even when there is no shared meaning or outwardly expressed value of being intuitive, you will find it in even the most conservative of environments.

Exercise 4:

Continue to focus on a situation you wish to resolve and release through the liberating process. You are now ready to invite a new reality through manifesting. The process is the same but in reverse.

1. Closing your eyes and taking a deep breath, bring your attention to your crown chakra. See that situation in the violet glowing disc just above your head. Invite in thoughts of the new reality you wish to create. It might be a new job, the beginning or end of a specific relationship, or another issue. Remember to use positive statements about what it is you do want. Think in present tense as if it is already so. Write about it in your journal.

2. Begin to move your attention downward through each chakra

   - see a new reality or perspective in how it might look moving forward (third eye)

   - give it voice to help create this new reality (throat)

   - feel it in your heart to know how it feels to be in right relations with the new situation (heart)

   - notice how it adds to your sense of personal power (solar plexus)

   - what pleasure or sense of well-being does this bring to you (sacral)

   - see it as already manifested in your life bringing greater sense of balance and grounding (root)

Mary Flanagan Gleason

Part V

WHAT NO LONGER SCARES ME

As my practice of liberating to manifest continues to inspire and challenge me, my thought process has changed dramatically. Understanding my intuitive nature has taken considerable pressure off me to live up to a different definition of success. Within my relationship with Mark, I learned to appreciate that we both fear different things and in different ways. I feel good about my hunches; where Mark goes crazy until there is enough data that often the moment for impactful decisions has passed. No decision feels right to him. He loves a high level of homeostasis.

Conversely, I leap without looking because I know there is a net there. I am more curious about dynamic shifts, running ahead to get a better look. I am easily overwhelmed when others demand details from me. It's not that I am a stranger to data nor am I incapable of getting it. I have held positions where I was frequently called upon to gather intelligence and present it in a coherent fashion. What rankles me is the dire need for copious amounts of data for even the smallest decisions. There isn't always time or need for such data gathering, and there isn't always data to support what I know to be true. This one detail – data—is scary to both of us: Mark's need for it and my angst at being dismissed if I don't have it.

Engineers learn to carefully diagram things out on paper and work it all through before beginning any project, a two-dimensional process. I get why that is. It is helpful when creating such amazing things as microchips, skyscrapers, transportation systems, or cars. Mistakes can be very expensive if you jump right in without having thought things through. Design thoughts are first simulated, measured, double-checked, and then evolve into a three-dimensional shape. It becomes external and can be validated step by step. I find it a fascinating process that leads to a different kind of knowing and absolutism that my hunches lack. My calculations come in glimpses and sensations and sometimes downright voices that steer me. They tend to be three or more dimensional, and yes, I know how that sounds. What it does not have is an external validation method that makes it possible for me to wait for everyone else to get comfortable before taking action. Sometimes the sense of urgency and frustration causes me to blurt out, "just trust me!" It is enough to scare someone of the more logical mindset because I can sound a little unhinged.

I love the Hermit tarot card. It reminds me of the value of going inside and, most importantly, to bring the light with us. So many logic-dominate sensors do not like that stuff. Let's just keep it all right here out in the open, out on the table, and look at the facts. Facts are good things, but they are not the only things. Worse, too, is that some facts are in the eye of the beholder. If you allow intuition to play at least a supporting role, you will see which facts hold water. By contrast, I have learned to love going inside knowing I will be greeted with truth, love, and respect. As my hypnotherapy clients come to appreciate, being greeted in this way makes it so much easier to acknowledge the limiting beliefs that need changing.

Mark loves a good road map. I do, too, but it isn't always necessary for me to have before I can explore new places. Mark makes the plan, measures, outlines the action steps, and double checks. Fear of the unknown is great, even with everyday stuff. Being unsure is scarier for Mark than for me.

On the other hand, Mark has always walked fearlessly into a crowd or a supermarket. He is happy to see people and assumes the best of most situations. On the other hand, I had to learn how much of other people's energy I was taking in. I would walk into the grocery store for a quart of milk and walk out with an unexplained sense of sadness, a sore knee, a headache, or, on rare occasions, feelings of elation. Learning that I was an empath was so helpful. Feeling others' emotions and pains in my body can be useful information but not if I am not aware it is not mine. It was so helpful to learn how to discern what was my pain and what belonged to another. I learned that I did not have to take on another's pain as my own and that things got better. Many alcoholics will tell you how helpful it is to learn about what it means to be empathic because so many have this trait in large doses.

This led to much of their anxiety. There are many reasons one is an alcoholic, but there are significant numbers that talk about how responsible they felt for other people's pain. There is a huge relief when you learn to recognize what belongs to you and what is just information.

I cannot say I feared going into stores and crowds because I am an extrovert. But, because I did not know what this sensing of others pain was, I can tell you that coming out of the store often led to the need for a nap, a pain reliever, or wondering why I felt so darn sad/happy/mad/worried. Once I learned that I am an empath and what that really meant, I learned to construct my bubble of protection.

A doctor told me many years ago that I was a sensitive. I thought he meant physically because I so readily responded to lower doses of medicine and because I experienced side effects often in just one or two doses of medicine. My body just knew what would and would not work. I realized later that this doctor was a medical intuitive, a sensitive, and he recognized the same in me. I had another doctor who openly laughed at me because I reacted so strongly to birth control pills in less than one week's dosage. He told me that it was not possible and that I was overreacting. Same profession yet one doctor was intuitive and one data-driven.

There is controversy about energetic bubbles in the intuitive community because people sometimes see them as impermeable. To me, it is all in how you construct it. My bubble allows information to come through that is for my greatest good or because Spirit needs me to relay a message. I missed a few of the messages but like everything else, it is a learned practice. My guess is that Spirit put the message out to too many people in the hopes that one of us will act on it. We are never alone. Nor were we meant to be the savior of others. We are merely one among many angels channeling information and performing acts of kindness.

I have an agreement with Spirit: honor my bubble. I have a bubble around me that can be penetrated by Spirit only if they have a message for me or need me to deliver a message. It works very well and keeps me from getting too depressed standing behind a stranger in the supermarket. The throat chakra oversees communication so when messages come through the bubble, I am being called to communicate, although it may also come with other sensations. The sensation may start with a feeling of pressure or pain somewhere, and when I open my mouth to speak, I hear the message for the first time as I speak it. That is channeling Spirit or a greater internal knowing.

On Friday mornings, I used to meet with a business networking group. We gathered for breakfast at a senior independent living community. The residents were very kind toward us and very respectful even though we were commandeering their dining hall for two hours each week. I held intuitive workshops there a few times and enjoyed connecting with the residents personally. One Friday, I walked in and placed my stuff at a table that was one floor below the residents' library. As I put my belongings by my seat, I felt a heavy sadness, an overwhelming sense of reluctant submission. I walked away to get my breakfast and the feeling disappeared. When I returned to the table the feeling of dread also returned. Okay, I thought, this feeling must be a message I am to deliver. I went to find the manager and asked her if there was someone in hospice care above that table. She said no, that it was the library, but there was a resident on hospice care just down the hall on the first floor. Then she lit up and said, "oh and she loves the library! She has read every book at least twice!" I said that Spirit had a message for this book lover in transition and proceeded to deliver a message I had heard for the first time as I spoke it: "Please tell her that when she passes, she can go to the library of her dreams and read any book she wants. Tell her she is going to a bigger and better library and not to worry about missing this one." The following week, the manager pulled me aside to say that with the family's permission they delivered the message. It wasn't too long afterwards that the resident passed away in complete peace. I love that Spirit used me that way.

Over the holidays, we went to do some touristy activities with visiting family. As we waited our turn in line and wandered through the gift shop, I felt it hard to breathe. It came and went in waves. Eventually, I told Mark what was happening in case I keeled over. It didn't dawn on me until later that night that I was picking up on someone else's illness. Since we spent the afternoon surrounded by the same tour group, it is possible the sensations came and went depending on a particular person's proximity. I knew then that I missed an opportunity to share a message from Spirit. I haven't a clue what it was, but it would have come forth once I made the connection. Sometimes I still get caught up in thinking the feeling is mine. Since COVID 19 arrived on the scene just a few months later, I wonder, too, if I was being warned to avoid someone who may be a carrier.

Using Affirmations

Affirmations are consciously made statements to aid in manifesting what we want to welcome into our world. Affirmations are best when written in the present tense as if what you wish to manifest is already done. When we say "everything will be good," that puts it out sometime in the future. When we say "everything is good," that puts it in the here and now. Spirit is ultimately a very positive presence and ignores negatives. Speak to what you want, not what you don't want.

When I first started, I posted a long list of affirmations on the bathroom mirror and read them aloud to myself twice a day. In that way, they became ingrained in the conscious mind. I found just the right one popping into my awareness in the middle of a conversation or thought process or situation that brought me back to center. One affirmation I repeated was, "I remain calm, centered, and peaceful regardless of anything." That one popped up over and over again as I worked to reclaim my life. It drew attention to forming my defensive stance, my thoughts preparing to go into battle rather than hear what the other person was saying. Powerful stuff.

If you are visually impaired, the power of speaking affirmations aloud is still important to manifesting them. If you are vocally impaired, write them down every day. Have them recorded and play the recording while you listen. Give them resonance until they become your truth. There are no limitations to access the power of the mind. Mentally and emotionally, we are always thoroughly equipped. I have included some affirmations at the back of the book to get you started. (See Appendix A)

Since our thoughts create our reality, our thoughts can also take us off course at any time. That is why we need a vision that continually brings us back to center. I work with so many nonprofits that desire help with their strategic planning process. The questions sometimes center around which step or goal is more appropriate. My answer is, "It depends on where you are trying to go." If you know where you are heading, the steps tend to fall into priority order, and unnecessary steps or distractions are easier to identify.

My life's vision includes traveling across America, Europe, Asia, Africa and a few spots in Central America. Best of all is if I can get paid to do it. In order to be most effective, it must be something that gives my life a sense of purpose and meaning while meeting the needs of others. I must be able to speak knowingly and with familiarity to this pain and offer something positive in return. Once I narrowed those topics down, the plan began to form. My step one: write this book. Share my journey to uncovering my intuitive self with others who may be experiencing a sense of enlightenment that is new and scary and who may be seeking community just as I did.

Personal visions become the litmus test for new and existing relationships as well as resource allocation, self-care, and where to spend one's time. To live into my goals, I need to liberate myself from codependent relationships that would clip my wings. Avoid lifestyle choices that might impact my health and spending precious resources on things that take away from my ability to do what I want to do. In *The Slight Edge*, Jeff Olson talks about the small things, the little individual tasks that we do or don't do that are the ones that ultimately add up to success. Not buying those really cute shoes is not a struggle if I cannot see how those shoes will get me closer to my vision. Spending less time playing computer solitaire gets easier when the litmus test is how it helps me finish my book, prepare for my next workshop or speaking engagement, or otherwise engage with my passions.

Couple's vision is a whole other realm. Mark and I worked with a financial planner who started the process with this simple question: "What do you envision for your retirement?" Given that we are in our 60's, this is no small consideration. It is not the first time we have explored this question but the answer changes as the reality of time sets in. I instantly talked about travel and indulging in more of my interests. On my vision board are places I want to see and where I dream of presenting workshops and participating in self-help and healing conferences. There are pictures of red rock canyons because they speak to my soul. I love to surround myself with them whether real or pictured. You will also see me superimposed on a TED talk stage, standing with Elizabeth Gilbert, and chatting with Oprah on Super Soul Sunday. I love Tony Robbin's quote, "Make a date with destiny or you will never get there." My vision board is my destiny. If I am not making progress toward those things, then I lessen the chances of realizing my vision. There is also a check made out to me for $1,000,000. Jim Carey had one for $10,000,000 on his vision board and it came to pass. I'm not limiting my dream to just a cool mil, though. Ten million is also welcome.

Mark, on the other hand, was frozen by this question of a vision. "How can I answer that when I don't know yet how much money I'll have?" My trying to explain that we could make investment decisions once we know the end game, was not helpful. In his mind, the strategy was obvious: Make lots of money. Once we know that, then we can plan. As the intuitive, I am all about living into the vision, and as the engineer, he is all about knowing exactly what the available resources will be. He will shrink his vision to stay more (utterly) practical if he must.

This disconnect causes tension as much as it inspires conversations to get in touch with what the other one is thinking. I never thought that I would be starting down a whole new career path at this stage in my life. It may seem foolish to some but to me it feels pleasantly unstoppable and a whole lot more practical than my friends who bought a puppy when their youngest headed off to college. I have found my zone of genius after so many years of living outside of it and I am excited to continue to live into it, full out.

The compromise comes in knowing that Mark will never spend two years in an RV on the road and I am not one to sit home for too long. Not wanting to travel as much is not the same as not wanting to travel at all. Wanting Mark to travel with me is not the same as wanting Mark by my side every minute. It turns out he is a really good podcast host so I'm planting vision seeds of him coming on the road with me, stopping to interview local breweries as we go. Sweetening the pot is legal in this process.

Exercise 5:

This next exercise involves the upper chakras beginning with the crown to create new thoughts, the third eye giving new perspective and ultimately, calling on the throat chakra of communication by writing it all down. The goal is to create a vision for yourself. Make it something just out of reach. Something you must strive to achieve. Most importantly, make sure it is true to you, regardless of your spouse or others. This is your vision, your dream. No one else gets a say in this important exercise unless you choose to invite them into your desired future.

Here is a meditation to use to guide you through this process. If you have someone who can read it to you, that is helpful, or perhaps you can make a recording of it to play while you meditate.

Find a quiet spot and a comfortable place to sit for the next 30 minutes.

- Pick a time in the future be it one year, two years, or five years. The goal is to imagine a positive life situation where you have arrived feeling good about yourself and life.

- Begin imaging that life at the very beginning of your day. When you wake up, notice where you are. You might be in your bed or you might be elsewhere.

- Notice who is or is not with you. Notice how you feel about it, remembering this is a positive state.

- What are you wearing? Is it sexy, comfortable, or even cozy? Maybe you are blissfully naked?

- Continue to move through your day one step at a time. What do you do when you wake up? Do you go for a walk, work out, eat a hearty breakfast? Be specific.

- It is time to get dressed. What will you wear? Is it a power suit for your role as CEO, biking outfit for your next 100-mile ride, swimwear for the beach, carefully selected clothes to wear to your TED talk? Walking shoes for a nature hike?

- What happens next? Where are you? Who is with you? How excited are you for this day?

- Lunch? What are you eating? Are you alone or with others? If there are others, who are they?

- In the afternoon, what does your schedule look like? A long hike, an exceptional presentation, a pedicure? Is anyone with you?

- Dinner time. Are you alone or with another or others? What are you eating? Where are you eating? At a restaurant, your mansion estate, your RV in the woods?

- At the end of the day, what are you most proud of? Grateful for?

Break down your day with as many details as possible. Relish each one. Notice how it all feels so you can recognize it during waking times. The goal is to really strive for that wonderful feeling of accomplishment.

Now write it all down in your journal including all the details. This calls on the throat chakra, the co-creator needed to manifest your dreams.

When you achieve vision for the future, take time to celebrate and then create a new vision. We should never stop creating or revising our vision for ourselves. Be BIG. Be bold. Be true to you.

Mary Flanagan Gleason

Part VI

THE GIFT OF OPPOSITION

The Edge Effect

The edge effect is where biodiversity scientists discover the newest life forms. It is at the end of two different biozones, such as forest and water. This concept is also where things like new sounds come from as musicians from different parts of the world come together, fusing cultures and instruments. The edge effect is a great way to consider how intuitives and engineers view things in new ways when they meet at the edge of their worlds. How much clearer is our understanding of the world when we come to the edge and dare to share?

When our youngest daughter graduated college, she was so full of information that she took to correcting us -- a lot. This is not out of the ordinary for a recent college grad, especially one who was such a great student. One day I suggested that she consider the difference between knowledge and wisdom. The former cannot become the latter without experience. The purpose of college is to present information and ideas to get you started in your adult life. The whole purpose of life is to face challenges and have experiences that turn that information into wisdom. The greater the challenge, the greater the learning. Being married to my opposite falls squarely under wisdom gathering. Learning that I am not stupid but smart in a different way was a huge lesson, one I could not have learned without the experiencing the resistance that is at the core of opposition, without walking to the edge to see what would happen. But it is not all upside.

When things do not overlap, when we come to the edge and things do not mesh well, it can cause real pain. I want to sell our house, throw our belongings in an RV and take off for parts unknown. Mark, on the other hand, always needs to know where home is. Each can get so frustrated by the other. Is it worth the marriage? I do not think that is what is at stake, but those discussions can get heated. During these times, we are obligated to check in with each other. Where else are we going to find another who shares and respects our history, our incredible journeys together and alone? Who will care about the same things to the same level that we each do? Who else will bear witness in the same way? There are other wonderful people out there, but let's face it, after more than thirty years of marriage, we are not going to have the same experience with another person. I have wondered on occasion that if I were single again, what kind of man I would find attractive. Oddly, I fear what things would be like if I were with someone who lives as much in the upper chakras as me. Someone has to fix the earthly stuff. Someone has to calculate and remember to pay bills. If left to my own devices, I can certainly do that. I have done so in the past. But hey, I like being married to a detailed engineer for many reasons, one of which is that these kinds of details are his nature. Can we survive separately? Of course. But why would we want to?

For Mark and me, energy serves as a point of alignment between the seemingly opposing approaches of intuitives and engineers. We both have studied it and are aware of its power. How we tap into it and the uses we put it to are often different, yet it is all based on the same premise: everything is energy.

Electrical engineers accept that there are things like invisible radio waves floating all around us in space. When properly tuned, you can channel your favorite radio station to the precise number on your dial. Those same principles apply to television. Your favorite sports and sitcoms dialed into a specific spot on your television. Where intuition challenges this understanding is in its limits to those things that humans put into the stratosphere. There is so much more than just radio and television waves and other human content. There are sound and light and energy ripples loaded with information. Engineering equipment is great for accessing human content. For me (and for you), my satellite dish is the crown chakra. Whenever I open my crown to scan frequencies, I am always amazed and humbled by what I can tune into. In the movie, Contact, I love Jodie Foster's character, an astronaut who finally gets to go into outer space. After a rough beginning, she finds she is floating in a world so beautiful it defies any language's ability to describe. Her scientific mind was overwhelmed. She whispers, "they should have sent a poet." For all of her extensive scientific knowledge and preparations, she was unprepared for how to articulate such beauty. I know how she felt. I often find access to amazing and even scary concepts, or what some people call receiving downloads, that inspire, inform, and overwhelm while defying language.

The Sacred is in the Mundane

When doctors graduate medical school, they go into medical practice, not perfection. We acknowledge that they have a good foundation and a certain level of intelligence and allow them to grow into their wisdom. As part of my journey, I have given myself that permission, too. I have much learning and experience to call upon, yet perfection is no longer the goal. Progress over perfection. Taking the time to be focused on the mundane as it correlates to the grander vision has brought another way to let go and allow. I offer that the sacred is in the mundane; the constant practice and little bits of learning and wisdom gathering that come throughout the journey.

From many different directions, I have had people encourage me to slow down. Chew slower, taste your food, stop and smell the roses, etc. Watching Mark tackle a project really drives my point home. He takes extra care to research, measure, and envision any project from one step to the next. When done, his work is impeccable, and the outcome is amazing. Gardening, building a birdhouse, brewing a craft beer, replacing a backyard fence. Slow, methodical, complete. Just how you want your organized world to be built and tended.

Waiting is not my strong suit. It is less about immediate gratification than a lack of ability to envision how things come together, one baby step at a time. I am a big picture person. I want to see what's possible. Reading The Slight Edge drove the point home in a different way, one I could hear and appreciate. Olson says that what you do with this moment matters to achieving your overall vision. Vision got my attention. If you want to lose ten pounds, then that one cookie sample at the store matters. If you want to be rich, what you do with one-dollar matters. If you want to write a book, what you do with your time everyday matters. He found my motivation: achieving my vision. I still eat too fast, but I am getting better at ignoring the urge to play computer solitaire. I embrace the mundane on my way to manifesting more extraordinary things.

To what degree is any one thing just one thing?

A relative of mine worked in a co-op called the NOTDOT Shop. It features items fashioned from recycled materials like purses made from old seat belts. Mostly, I love what the name stands for: No One Thing Does One Thing. Regardless of our dominant traits, everyone has times when we call on our less dominant skills. Everyone is intuitive.

Mark is a dominant five senses kind of guy, yet he is a very intuitive gift giver. Long before I understood my intuitive side, Mark gave me gifts like the book The Botany of Desire. He just thought I might like it. At the time, I was confused, but now I know it was something he saw in me before I did. Mark has always been good like that. He does that kind of magical, insightful thing for a lot of people. He finds things they did not know they wanted but loved receiving. I come from a family of dominant intuitives, but we are very practical gift givers; gift cards and sweaters whose colors won't show the dirt - that sort of thing. But I am not sure you can nurture someone into being more intuitive as much as recognize the different ways it shows up. It is not that Mark is not intuitive at all; he simply has a natural learning preference for things with heft and dimensions. To Mark, intuitive gift giving "just makes sense."

I have yet to meet a person who does not have some intuition or does not call on their other five senses. The trick is to be aware of what is most dominant for you and embrace your nature rather than allow your gifts and perspective to be considered less valuable. I am so grateful that Mark can see the pieces I cannot, and I know he has benefited from my perspectives even if he did not understand at first. One thing about being intuitive is that when new ideas bubble to the surface, we embrace the message more quickly, and then we go get the details.

On occasion, I can fix things. About two years into our first new home, both outdoor lights attached to either side of the garage went out. Mark instantly started following the wiring figuring something serious must be wrong. Why else would they go out at the same time? I suggested changing the light bulbs. After all, they were put in at the same time, they always go on at the same time, so my guess was we needed to change both bulbs. After finding nothing wrong with the wiring, he reluctantly replaced both bulbs. It worked. We laugh about this now, but it has become code for overthinking a problem. "Are you replacing the wiring before trying a new bulb," I'll ask. He is a good sport and will often lighten up on the intensity of the situation. Occasionally, he will invoke Occam's Razor, a philosophy that proposes that the simplest solution is often the correct one as a gentle reminder to himself. It also reminds me that having too much information can be a curse.

I always thought Mark's need for details was his way of saying "no." Of resisting what I was saying. Now I know he was asking for more information to help him understand. I no longer feel crushed under the weight of getting all the details for Mark, but I have learned he cannot move forward on any project or decision without them, and so I must allow time for him to gather them. I have also learned that when he puts a project off for long periods, he is unsure of how to do the task at hand. In a world designed by engineers, that is a good trait.

No Surprises!

If you have already tried this with your dominant sensor, then you know: never throw a detailed planner-type a surprise party. Successful, well trained engineers are strict planners. I asked Mark to tell me his ideal fortieth birthday party, which he did. Then I called on one of his golfing buddies, and we pulled it together. In hindsight,

Mark gave me only the big picture and none of the details. As you can imagine, I got a lot of things wrong but none more wrong than surprising him. I am the spontaneous one. As I get older, the thought of big parties does not hold the same appeal. I would rather spend the money on travel. So, while we seem to be the same page now, it is really me who has changed my priorities. Neither of us has changed our stripes.

In his book, *The Rational Psychic*, Jack O'Rourke talks about how being psychic is not a real thing because everyone has access to the information. To him, it is not a mystery; it is a choice. He has always been able to see, hear, and know things. He has always conversed with those who have passed or even not in the same room. Doesn't everyone? It seems rather logical to him. For a long time, I was mystified by his reasoning since it was a new-found skill for me. It was during the writing of this book that I got it. I realize now that what I see, know, and hear isn't obvious to all. I am more in tune with this level than the seventy-five percent of the population grounded in the five physical senses. Mark, too, thinks that what he knows is obvious and I am resisting logic. He was waiting for me to catch up, catch on, dive in the way he does. Mark has come to understand that I am not going to think the way he does, and I get that he truly does not see, know, or hear things the way I do. I need him to do the math, find the best route, break down projects, and he needs me to remind him of the power of positive manifestation by envisioning a grander future and warn that a certain house is not built right.

I love teaching people as they discover how their intuition shows up for them. It is not uncommon to hear from students that they thought intuition or being psychic was something other than what they experience. Because a certain way is not true for that individual, they believe they are not intuitive. For example, one woman told me that she did not think she was intuitive because she only hears things. It was her understanding that being psychic meant seeing things, prophesying the future. Now she knows that clairaudience (clear hearing) is her intuition. It is a much stronger knowing for some of us, while it is more subtle for others. It is also accepting it as intuition. I would often hear song lyrics or see scenes from movies and think, "how random." Weirder still was when something related to that would happen. Now I know that it was my earliest glimmers into the intuitive realm. However, the biggest difference is how well it works when you take the time to listen to it. If your gut is your primary warning system, you do not have to have anyone else tell you to trust it. Nor do you need to wait until it gets your attention with a five-alarm fire. You can purposefully stop in the moment and check in with it.

- How does my gut feel about this situation or decision?
- Is it a little upset or completely relaxed?
- Does the energy feel contracted or expansive?
- Is it warm or too hot?

If that is your intuition, trust it. It is the only thing that is for your greatest good and highest purpose. Call on your intuition for any decision, big or small. In the morning, I stop and consider each breakfast option in my mind and wait to see what my stomach says. It will tell me by a twinge, a neutral feeling, or an outright burning sensation which option is right for me today.

Accuracy versus Flow

Sometime around the third date with my husband, I challenged him to tell me what he wanted to say without drawing it on a cocktail napkin. He would outline the cubicle layout in his office to demonstrate that the person he was referring to sat diagonally across from him. So often, details like where the person sat were not necessary for me to understand the story. He would do this to explain a near miss in traffic, drawing street layouts with an X for his car and O for the on-coming offender. Eventually, I gave up, realizing it was the same as if he had asked me to refrain from using my hands when I talked and deny generations of my Irish-Italian upbringing.

For Mark, it is the exactness of his story that matters. For me, it is the emotion and elegance of the story. He prefers to read cookbooks and scientific articles, and I much prefer novels and self-help books. How I love a good story well told. Characters, plots, adventures, realizations. He prefers information told in a logical sequence with accuracy and attention to detail. We, his loving family, tease him that when we ask him a question, could he just give us the answer without starting at the Big Bang and working forward. Alas, teasing Mark is all fun and games until something needs fixing and where an elegant story of its brokenness will not suffice.

When we discuss pretty much anything, we continue to come at the subject from our distinct positions. The blessing is how much we learn from each other and see this as a blessing. I often wonder how I might be a homeowner without someone who thinks like Mark. The math alone would kill me. I am blessed that at least one of us knows how to do this stuff.

Downsizing

If it were up to me, we would have downsized our house several years ago. The idea, however, has met with great resistance from Mark and for reasons not without merit. Once I acknowledged the financial and relocation issues, there was still something not sitting well with Mark. Not one to let things drop, I pushed until Mark finally expressed something I had never considered. Mark is more deeply rooted in this house than I am. He has touched just about every board and wall in ways I have not. Many of the nails that hold things together were placed there by his hands. He built a shed to make more room for his very fulfilling life in the garage. Some repairs are a reminder of his ingenuity. The yard is a reflection of all his creativity, care and labor. Mark doesn't want to lighten his load. He loves his load.

Now I know how it is received when I only half-jokingly suggest that we should not buy anything for the house that will not fit in an RV. While he led with the numbers (and they were correct, as usual), somewhere I was suggesting that all his labor and things that ground him were easily transportable. It was not my intention, but it still happened. It is his heart, solar plexus, his sacral and root chakras at stake: his air, his fire, his pleasure, his roots, all he has proudly made manifest in his life. I still want to downsize, but I know now that there will be a yard and enough room for his brewing equipment wherever we land next. The RV will be more of an occasional excursion, no doubt when the ground is too wet to garden, and warmer climates call to us. I will have to find other ways to satisfy my upper chakra desire to be free to follow what resonates with me and to give birth to new visions in new ways. I will not surrender them, but I have to remember that how I proceed has an impact on Mark.

Masculine and Feminine

Intuition or yin is considered a feminine trait regardless of the individual's gender. Yang is considered masculine also regardless of physical gender. In the Tao of Physics (1983 edition), author Fritjof Capra writes, "Our culture has consistently favored yang, or masculine, values and attitudes and has neglected their complementary yin, or feminine counterparts." That statement feels validating to me. What other traits do we regard as masculine? I would include physical power, the ability to make things tangible and accessible, the ability to dominate a situation or another person. It implies that if someone is not physically afraid of me, or if I am not able to express myself specifically and with data, I am no threat and everything about me is taken less seriously. This cultural norm Capra describes is not Universal law, therefore it is not a waste of time for me to step into my intuition and own it as a powerful necessity.

Capra went on to say, "We have favored self-assertion over integration, analysis over synthesis, rational knowledge over intuitive wisdom, science over religion, competition over cooperation, expansion over conservation, and so on. This one-sided development has now reached an alarmingly high stage, a crisis of social, ecological, moral, and spiritual dimensions. However, we are witnessing, at the same time the beginning of a tremendous evolutionary movement."

Hallelujah! Capra wrote this book about the time I stumbled on to Jonathan Livingston Seagull. While I was just beginning to awaken even the slightest bit, he was writing this call to arms. The world needs us. Intuitives unite!

I once did a workshop for forty-five CEOs and CFOs of major nonprofits. They represented organizations with minimum budgets of $40M. They were not small organizations, and their leaders were talented and experienced managers. The workshop was titled, "Bring Your Whole Brain to Work." I asked the group "who here has had that interview candidate that was perfect on paper, had excellent references yet left a nagging feeling in the pit of your stomach?" Every hand went up. I continued. "And, after much rationalizing and reviewing of the paperwork, you hired them anyway?" Again, every hand. Then I asked, "and how many of them turned out to be a real problem in the organization?" Again, every hand. So, then I asked how such smart people can have this happen to them?

For the next hour and a half, I led them through a series of small exercises to get in touch with their intuition at a high level and apply it to a real situation they are currently facing. Did it make a difference to how they saw the situation and the solution?

When the exercises were applied to the situation involving hiring the wrong person, participants could see how the right brain was trying to tell them that all is not right with this candidate. How much aggravation and money could it have saved to either re-examine the other candidates or restart the search?

Afterward, one CEO stopped me in the hallway and said, "the whole time I could feel my wife slugging me in the arm saying, 'I told you so." Again, that feminine energy being sidelined in favor of the quantifiable rather than being considered as a full partner in the decision. Some talked about the inability to express their hunches in reasonable ways prevented them from listening. In other words, they were afraid of being seen as irrational or "woo-woo." And yet, so many of the top business leaders in the world talk about following their intuition when making business decisions. The right and the left brain, the yin and the yang, exist in harmony to keep us balanced and fully informed. Bad decisions cost money and time, the two resources most precious to any business. When I work with executives, I often spend time helping them tap into their intuition, encouraging them to recognize how it shows up for them and value it as an equal partner in making decisions. I further encourage them to lead by inviting their staff to incorporate intuition as part of the decision-making process. It only takes a minute to do and can save hundreds of hours and thousands of dollars down the road.

I just want to underscore that I am not saying that one's intuition should overrule the data. I am saying you will do better to make it an equal partner. Sometimes, a nagging feeling may encourage you to get more data, not necessarily to say no to something.

The Left and Right Brain

Dr. Jill Bolte Taylor is a neuroanatomist (brain scientist) researching the brain's map to better understand mental illness. She wrote My Stroke of Insight, detailing the massive left sided stroke she suffered at only 37 years old. She spent the next two years accessing only the right side of her brain, relying on intuition and energy to make sense of her world. She reports that while she could not physically recognize anyone and had no concept of language, she could tell who to trust by their energy. Her mother's energy was warm and loving, and she welcomed it into her hospital room. By contrast, she became agitated at the unfamiliar energy of the custodian, a total stranger. She noted that everyone's energy is far greater than the size of their physical body. Bolte Taylor goes on to say that she was amazed at the amount of information she had ignored all her life and how it will forever impact her research and understanding of what we call mental illness. In fact, a person just may be more greatly in touch with their right brain, not always able to reason it through with left brain assistance like language and mathematics. She had a rare opportunity to consciously experience life from each hemisphere's perspective, one at a time.

Eastern and tribal cultures have long seen people we call mentally ill as prophets. They recognize their right-brained life and do not expect them to be grounded or fit in a sensory dominant world. They act to provide grounding for them. In terms of manifesting, I was struck by Dr. Bolte Taylor's strong desire and verbalized intention to understand mental illness and how Spirit responded. One might say, "be careful what you ask for," while hindsight might say "Oh, yes. Now I see. Thank you." Everything is always for your greatest good and highest purpose, always in the highest order of light and love.

Nature versus Nurture

There are no compromises with Mark's and my different natures, only recognizing that we are both needed in this world. Each of us receives insights from the other's perspective. We do an injustice when we discount how the other makes sense of their world and insist it be our way. The best path to understanding is to lean in, ask more questions, believe the answer even if you do not understand it, or even buy into it. We can be sensitized and allow ourselves to be nurtured, but that will never replace our nature.

In my career pathing, I focused on getting promotions to higher and higher levels of responsibility. Every promotion got me tied tighter to my desk and away from what I most loved; working with donors and building connections between them and the organizations I served. Budgets and timelines and management concerns were my nurture; I learned how to do those things over time. Building relationships was my nature and the further away I got from that, the more unhappy I became.

Exercise 6

Note in your journal where you find opposition in your life. It can be a situation, a person, a job, a household need, etc. How does each instance make you feel? What skills do you need to work through it? Ask yourself:

- Is this really mine to worry about?
- Can I realistically change this?
- Is something or someone acting in opposition to me or is it a reaction to something about it or them?
- Where is the gift? What have I learned?

Remember that opposition can simply be calling attention to your next level of personal growth and understanding of your world.

That is not to say that all opposition is worth your time and energy. Sometimes we find where it is better to drop the rope and walk away. Sometimes we come to recognize and appreciate something new that adds to our life.

Part VII

THE RESEARCH

I did a lot of research to make my point about the intelligence of intuition, power behind it, and the need for it in everyday life. It was exhilarating for me to think that I – my form of intelligence - could be validated in the Muggle world. I wanted to show the engineers in my life (which living in a high-tech part of the country is the majority of people I know) the science behind the way my brain works. What I found was that for every scientific report, there is one more standing behind it to disprove all or some of it. Then I realized that is pretty much true of any topic you research. It is like going to Yelp and finding that fifty percent of reviews are raves, and fifty percent are rants. Nothing relieves you of the responsibility to decide for yourself. Intuition works for me. My own life experiences are all the research I need to know. When I live outside of that deep inner knowing, life attacks. When I live within it, life flows. Still, reading the reports and studies, I found it fulfilling and validating that others know of the existence and importance of intuition, enough so to study it.

Waiting for Science to Catch Up

I want to acknowledge all the amazing scientists and artists who had incredible visions of what is possible and then documented them to share with others. I sometimes see pieces of my journey reflected in theirs, if even just a little. It makes me feel that sense of community I sometimes otherwise miss in the engineered world.

I fell in love with Dr. Bruce Lipton's research explained in his book, *The Biology of Belief*. His research underscores my experience: the power of the mind is the greatest power of all. Our mind holds the greatest curative powers or conversely, the greatest destructive powers. Dr. Lipton shook up old scientific beliefs about the "99.9 percent empty space" in a cell, proving that it is not empty but full of energy that responds to thoughts, sounds, language, and environment. Just like our souls. Just like our human selves. What he discovered flies in the face of big pharma, which spends billions of dollars trying to convince us that our greatest cure is a tablet or liquid that we must purchase and ingest. It simply would not bode well if we found out that the placebo effect is equally effective and sometimes more so than external medicine. Mark thinks the placebo effect somehow makes fools of us. My only concern is if I feel better. If changing my thoughts will do the trick, then, why wouldn't I?

Dr. Joe Dispenza outlines his discovery of the mind's power in his book, *You Are the Placebo*. Dr. Dispenza is a neuroscientist who first became a chiropractic doctor after healing himself from a violent motorcycle accident where the options doctors gave him were all horrible and would leave him paralyzed. He chose instead to use the power of the mind to envision his body healing one bone, one tendon at a time, until he could walk and move almost as easily as if it had never happened. It took a very long time, but as he notes, time was all he had. In the end, his mind healed him and continues to keep him moving today. He is living proof of the power of being intuitively connected to his body, yet he is seen as "alternative" and "woo woo." I cannot think of stronger evidence except that science requires more data. Our society continues to reject our individual power even after such a tangible demonstration. It is not the power of Dispenza's brain that is exceptional. It's that he tuned into the stamina and determination that many of us abandon when things get hard or are not happening fast enough or runs up against a misguided belief that we cannot be successful. Or we remain stuck in our victim's story. We default to "tried that. Didn't work. Poor me. Somebody else will have to do it."

Artists are amazing at channeling and manifesting. I believe it was Mozart who said that he never created a composition; he just wrote it down as it came through him. His crown chakra was wide open as he channeled with the great advantage of language to scribe these incredible downloads. Michelangelo looked at a slab of marble and said that he chiseled away anything that was not the subject. He could see the finished product contained in the rock. Intuition comes from the same part of the brain as creativity. I see things, know things, am inspired by things that I cannot describe, draw, or otherwise communicate in ways that will meet the dominant sensor's standards. In that way, I can be seen as quite inept. Yet, I stand by my intelligence and live into my strengths which is in sticking to what I know, however I know it.

When I work with clients on liberating what holds them back to manifest a better way of life, I am consciously aware of the fallacy of empty space. When we liberate what no longer serves, we free up space in our physical, mental, and emotional being. The Universe cannot allow a void. It rushes in to fill it. My clients' responsibility to consciously fill it with what works for them is immense and vital and all kinds of powerful. When a client experiences that sweet understanding and release of old stories that hold them back, they are so excited! They often jump up from their trance state and feel ready to take on the world. "I feel so light! Like a huge weight has been lifted!" It is a joyous dance that I indulge for a few minutes. Then I insist they continue by inviting what they would like to welcome into that space that will bring them joy and serve them better.

I had a client, a woman in her late 50's, who was tired of being depressed. She had been treated for her depression, starting in young adulthood and worked with a number of therapists to find the root cause. Then she decided to try hypnotherapy to see if the cause was something from a past life that followed her into this lifetime. I guided her to a doorway behind which she would find the answer. In the interest of confidentiality, I will only say what she found scared her, and we spent a good amount of time making her feel safe enough to continue. Finally, she could take a step back and see the whole situation clearly before her. She was witnessing her birth and noticed her mother and father were not the joyous parents you might expect. Her father was stern and distant, and her mother was overwhelmed, exhausted, and definitely not in love with her husband. As she sat cradled in her mother's arms, she watched as she absorbed her mother's dark cloud of depression. This brand new, defenseless bundle of sentience absorbed her mother's depression. Realizing what had happened, she jumped up in relief at discovering it was not her depression! She did not need to own it. What a relief!

Almost as quickly as the relief flooded in, so, too, did the guilt. She felt she was somehow abandoning her mother. So, I asked if her carrying the depression all these years meant her mother wasn't depressed. "Oh, no. She's never been happy." So, I further reasoned that her being depressed only meant that two people were unhappy instead of one? "Yes, I guess that's true." I then asked if she would like to keep the depression. "No!" She sat back down, closed her eyes, and released it with a great exhale. As she felt the relief, I asked her what she wanted to do with her newfound sense of well-being. She said, "I want to retire and travel." I encouraged her to experience how such things would make her feel and invite that feeling to fill the space once occupied with sadness. Her entire face changed. More relaxed, fewer wrinkles, softer. She fell into a bit of sleep for a minute. When she woke, she could not believe how much lighter she felt.

Please note that this was not an instant cure. She still had to allow this new information to inform her actions toward her mother. She needed to make very conscious decisions about how she wanted to show up differently. It is also important to note that I do not think she would have gotten such startling results without her years of therapy. She had to eliminate all the other possibilities first before she could trust this insight. None of what we do to better understand ourselves is wasted.

Many clients want to end self-sabotaging behaviors like overeating or smoking. Often the client's understanding is limited to the behavior. Suppose they don't also work on consciously creating what will work better for them. In that case, it is pretty much a guarantee that they will take up a different self-sabotaging behavior while patting themselves on the back because they are not doing the first thing they addressed. Simply not overeating might lead to shopping sprees. Quitting smoking might lead to excessive nail-biting. Not drinking might lead to pot smoking or over-controlling everything else to avoid the triggers that led them to drink. To relieve yourself of one behavior without addressing the reason, the underlying cause, does nothing to relieve your mind's need to continue to self-harm. Something else slides into that empty space. Best that you choose it in ways that are self-loving, gentle, easy to call on. This is where affirmations are helpful. Affirmations can help gently and positively keep you focused on a calm and more desirable way to go through the day.

Clients who overeat often report they joined a Weight Watchers group. Here they learn to count calories, discuss how well they did at the party by avoiding the cake, etc. This tells me how much they are caught up in will power. Will power leaves you in constant fight mode, always focused on resisting what you don't want rather than moving toward what you do want. When a client can address why they overeat with compassion for themselves, it is much more effective. When I quit smoking with the help of hypnosis, I realized that I used smoking as a literal smokescreen to keep my boss out of the office. I found it equally helpful and much healthier to close my door with a sign that said, "on deadline." Running off to the gym at lunchtime also kept her at bay.

Bending Spoons and the Power of Thought

No matter how much I studied metaphysics, there was one feat I could not achieve: bending spoons. A colleague was doing an introductory class to metaphysics and bending a spoon was part of the class. The basic, entry-level class! I was intrigued so I attended because clearly, I was missing something basic. Toward the end of class, we each got a spoon and a few instructions, and then... I did it! I bent the spoon! Not with brute force but with my thoughts. Now, if you're like many in my family you may want to yell something like, "it's science!" to which I say, "duh!" And yet, it is so much more.

Here's the science behind spoon bending: The power is in your thoughts, controlling the flow of energy from inside. In that moment of success, I had closed my eyes and visualized energy flowing from my heart through my left arm, and then my right, forming a continuous loop in both directions passing through the fingers positioned on the neck of the spoon. Remember that the heart chakra is where all the chakras meet up. I borrowed from my thoughts through the crown above, my declared determination through the throat chakra above, and the fire from the solar plexus below. As per the instructions, I focused only on the flow of energy and the increasing heat generated by my solar plexus (personal power) and circulated through my heart. Within just a few minutes, I noticed the spoon was loosening and I bent it back with very little pressure. It bent to my will. If I can do this with a spoon, what other situations might change in my favor if I direct my energy in a concentrated way? Here's the bottom line: Bending a spoon has nothing to do with the spoon. It has to do with where you focus your internal energy.

I recently read about someone's first white-water rafting lesson: those new to the sport are aware of the rocks. Skilled rafters are aware of the water's flow. In this instance, I initially focused on bending the spoon, but I had not changed my perspective. I had to learn to shift my energy and my thoughts in a new way to get different results. When I finally learned to focus on generating energy in a focused way, I was in the flow, and the rest gave way for my desired outcome. These days, when I am feeling stuck on an issue (or maybe in a tug of war with Mark on some issue or another), I bend a spoon. It reminds me of the power of shifting my thoughts and energy. Not that Mark will bend to my will. Heavens, no! But in doing so, it reminds me that there are many ways to look at a situation, many ways I can choose to use my energy. If I am not getting the results I want, there is every chance I will do better if I can shift my focus. I choose to focus on the flow.

Exercise 7

Bend a spoon.

Find a spoon of normal thickness at the neck, the place on the handle just above the tines. Hold the neck of the spoon gently in front of you between your thumbs and forefingers. Now, close your eyes and envision your inner energy flowing in an uninterrupted loop from your core, down your right arm, through the spoon neck, into your left arm back to your heart. Once that energy is flowing, picture a simultaneous energy loop from your core going through the left arm, around through to the right arm. and back to the core. Allow these two energy streams to continue for as long as you need to, keeping your mind focused only on running the energy. You may find that you will begin feeling warm, possibly overheating. Every now and then, give the spoon a slight test to see if it is ready to bend easily. Hint: I get a bag of spoons from the area thrift shop. They usually have eight to ten spoons for $1.

Note in your journal what that felt like. If you cannot get the spoon to bend the first time, try again later. Try as many times as it takes. It may help to practice in private or with a supportive person rather than making it a performance or contest of some kind. This exercise is all about harnessing your internal power.

Journal your experiences. Find the parallels in your daily life to this exercise. Where are you experiencing something that, if you could change the shape of it, or bend back the edges, it would work better for you? How can you step into that power by directing your energy in new ways?

Part VIII

GREAT AHA MOMENTS

Manifesting Community

When I was pregnant, I could not believe how many other women were also pregnant. We were everywhere. When I broke my wrist, it seemed as if every other person had a cast. They were there all along, but I did not see them until it was personal to me. My spiritual awakening was and is like that. I realized I am not alone, that others had similar awakenings, and still others are already here, on my path to guide me. The same was true when I learned to read tarot cards, I began to see the symbols everywhere: in movies, advertisements, artwork. Everywhere. If I want to manifest something new, it seems that merely thinking about it brings it into my realm.

Such was the case when I allowed Spirit to guide me to my computer and search for opportunities to develop my intuition. I found the teacher, and I found a whole group who wanted to do the work with me. Voila! Community. When I wanted to start a business centered on my intuitive skills, I found my business networking group who introduced me to a business coach. I thought this coach would focus on business building, but she started by insisting each of us in the group truly understand our Myers Briggs Type Indicator. Almost everyone in this group of 35 women was dominantly intuitive. More community! I was also amazed to find so many books, spiritual bookstores, workshops, presentations, EVERYWHERE! They were all waiting for me and welcomed me with open arms. None of this could have happened if I had not first let go of what was no longer serving me. I had to make room for something better. I feared I would be alone, and now I know I was just in the wrong community. And then, of course, I realized how many other times these same opportunities had crossed my path before, but I didn't see them until now. I was never really alone.

I Knew It All Along

I could have told you some of the messages behind children's stories, but as my understanding of symbolism grows, I realize how many of these messages have been available to me from an early age. This means that many others before me saw the world as I do now and found a way to share it. My two all-time favorite childhood stories are Peter Pan and The Wizard of Oz.

I remember watching Peter Pan on television. It was a huge event, and it sucked me in like the six-year-old sponge that I was. Mary Martin played Peter Pan, and he could fly. Additionally, Peter Pan was a malcontent who broke all the rules and still brought order as a leader of the Lost Boys, those boys without a mother. They lived in Neverland. Peter Pan appeared in the Darling Household nursery to recruit the oldest child, Wendy, to be the boys' mother. They so deeply craved that connection to the feminine. Pan offered to take Wendy and her two younger brothers to Neverland to meet the boys, but first, they had to learn to fly. What has always resonated in my soul is when the youngest of the Darling children, Michael, was having trouble learning to fly. He could not get any lift despite his older siblings' quick mastery. He assumed it was because he was too little, but it was his thinking holding him down. When Peter Pan suggested that Michael needed to think lovely thoughts, he had to stew on them for a while. Then they came flooding in: Birthdays? Presents? Christmas!" And off Michael went!

I get that now in a whole new way. When I feel down, too grounded, stuck, I know my thoughts need addressing. Changing my thoughts lightens my perspective. I feel like I can fly. Depression is a function of the crown chakra where thoughts are paramount. I must ask myself:

- Why do I believe I cannot or should not do something?
- Where am I deferring to others' comfort?
- Why am I feeling stupid?
- What am I afraid of?

The situation around me may be dour and not of my making, but my thoughts will determine my ability to lift myself out of the chaos. A simple example is when I have to do technical things on the computer. I can feel my stomach tense (restrained personal power, ego afraid of failing) just thinking about the impending task. I may even blow up while reading instructions that I do not understand. I feel frustrated and angry and incredibly stupid, like the world is moving on without me. It is in moments like these that I must change my thoughts: "You are smart enough to figure this out. Give yourself the time and patience you show your clients." A personal favorite is to say, "you are smart enough to ask for help."

Another favorite scene in Peter Pan is when Tinkerbell's light begins to dim. She drank the poison intended for Peter as a sign of love. (Ugh! How many times did I take on other people's problems?!) As a result, she became sluggish, and her ability to respond grew faint. Peter Pan encourages everyone to help Tinkerbell grow bright again by clapping. "Clap as loud as you can so she knows that you believe in fairies - in her!" Of course, I clapped my fool hands off and felt personally responsible for saving a life when her light returned. She quickly resumed flying around, sprinkling fairy magic everywhere. Words of affirmation is my love language. Clapping and encouragement work for me, too. Life has taught me that applauding works well for most people. Sometimes I must ask people to clap for me. Sometimes I clap for myself. Either way, my light shines brighter. I wanted to believe I was Peter Pan because he could fly but I was really Tinkerbell giving away my power while I remained the size of a small blip of light. Please do not applaud anyone drinking another's poison.

Most powerfully, though, in my earliest days of meditating and unlocking the door to all this incredible wisdom, I kept hearing Glinda the Good Witch from The Wizard of Oz gently chiding me: "You've always had the power, my dear. You just had to learn it for yourself." The power, the solutions, the understanding, and the ability to see a future were all right here, in my gut that had been leaking. In my third eye, that lost perspective. In my thoughts that were focused on all the wrong things. You and I were born with unfettered access to Divine wisdom. We meet tigers and lions and bears along the way. Even flying monkeys make an occasional appearance. They are our fears and imagined boogeymen that keep us small and afraid of expanding our energy. It was the ruby slippers (root chakra) that brought Dorothy back home to her roots after believing that whatever she craved was somewhere over the rainbow when in fact, it was right in her own backyard. Unlike me, Dorothy was a fast learner. She only needed a bump on the head.

When I had hit rock bottom, it was time to rebuild. Armed with a new understanding of me and my actions, I felt as if my world was so much more manageable, and my role in the world was still in its infancy. Contrary to my fears, time had not run out. The man behind the curtain reflected my victim's story believing that someone else would rescue me. In all of my rescuing of others, I acted out what I wanted the world to do for me. It turns out the Wizard was just as lost as Dorothy. They worked together in empathy and compassion to get home. That's when Glinda appeared, commending Dorothy for her diligence and offering that she had always had the power. Dorothy did not need rescuing. She only needed to tap into her own wisdom, to own her own power. To recognize she was never really lost at all. She met amazing characters along the way but ultimately, she no longer needed them the way she once envisioned. (As a side note, each of those characters also found what they thought they lacked already existed inside them, too. They were also looking for external validation.) I feel that way about my collection of friends and jobs that were what I thought I wanted but didn't really serve me.

My fire began to burn brightly again, but this time in a good way. Sometimes I call on the tarot Hermit card to bring forth the light while I go inward. People get so afraid of going inward because of the darkness. Like me, they worry about what they might find. Even worse, it means confronting all we successfully secreted away. The Hermit reminds me that the darkness can only be relieved by light. So, I go inward, inviting Divine white light to accompany me. One of my earliest revelations about stuffing scary things down, such as my true feelings, is how much room they take up. When I finally shared my deepest feelings with a therapist, I could not believe how small they were when compared to the bigger picture. Inside is very cramped, so small things feel huge and uncomfortable. When we move those same things to a bigger space, like the space outside of us, we can see how small they really are. How much more manageable.

The Harry Potter book series was another surprising new-found sense of community. For example, we both had trouble relating to the Muggle (engineered) world. My favorite part was Hogwarts, the School of Wizardry and the Room of Requirement. As the name implies, everything we need is already provided to us. Always has been. We simply need to name what it is we need and allow it to come to us.

Who knew? I mean, besides Glinda and all the mystics and writers of children's stories? My power was not over the rainbow but contained in the rainbow of the chakras, right here inside me, and I would not ignore it any longer. Your power is there, too. Ignoring it can make you sick.

Be Careful Whose Approval You Seek

"Be careful whose approval you seek for they become your captors."
- Buddha

If like me, your love language is Words of Affirmation, this can be a real problem. Words of affirmation is just one of five "love languages" spelled out in Gary Chapman's book, *The Five Love Languages: The Secret to Love that Last*s. (The other languages are Receiving Gifts, Acts of Service, Quality Time, and Physical Touch.) Words of affirmation means that I respond well to being recognized, appreciated, and complimented. Since this type of affirmation typically comes from another, I put myself in the position of becoming another's captive. In truth, the one person who needs to approve of me is me. Once I give that to myself, needing it from others is less imperative although still very much welcome. Most people do not want the job of having to constantly affirm another, yet they hold all kinds of power by merely wanting it. The number one person who holds one captive is self. I must stop and consider very deeply

- Why do I need something so seemingly imperative from another?
- Where are my self-doubts coming from?
- Why am I withholding approval from myself?
- Is it a new situation for which I do not have the information?
- Is it information I can research? Where are the experts that can provide insights to help me then decide if I am doing well?

These are different than the overwhelming need for approval. I must approve of me, even when (especially when) I make a mistake. What is a mistake anyway? Sometimes it is falling into an old pattern, usually involving cynicism and sarcasm. I am too quick to judge or do not stop to consult my intuition before acting. That is when I get into the most trouble.

Forgiveness and gratitude go hand in hand with self-approval. They are the keys to letting oneself off the mat and changing thoughts. There were far too many times when I could not sleep with the thought that I had made a mistake, feeling exposed in some horrible way. I had received many compliments throughout my career and even personal life for how well I handled something in the moment. Still, I would go home and obsess over how I should have done it differently. Or when I would ask a question of a presenter in a conference room full of peers and I would fret all night thinking how I just revealed how much I do not know. The sense of vulnerability was so great that I would stew in my shame. It was equally amazing how often no one else even paid attention or cared.

But most importantly, I can feel my own growth at how very little I do that nowadays. I allow myself to have questions, not to understand, and give myself credit whenever I ask for clarity. I am grateful for how often I receive new information and grateful for the time others take to respond to queries. Moving from feeling exposed and vulnerable to open to receiving with genuine gratitude for others' willingness to teach has been a game changer.

Don't Take Life Personally

When I was a child, I remember one time when my mother was on the phone with a friend. When she hung up, I asked what she was talking about. Adult things, she answered. Then I asked what I really wanted to know, which was if she was talking about me. My mother very casually mentioned that she had more than just me in her life to discuss. I was flabbergasted. Sometimes I harken back to this earlier time to remind myself that another person's life is about them, not me. Just like my life is about me, not them.

As an adult, I think that inner childishness rises to the surface. Someone's irrational response to a question usually means they are having a bad day. I have come to learn from my mother, co-workers, and even my dear husband, that irrational behavior is often the result of a bad day. Their bad day. Taking it personally is futile and very woe-is-me. Maybe I need to let the comment go altogether or maybe I need to wait a bit and then circle back to ask if everything is okay.

But how often did I take it as them reacting to me and my actions? There were many tugs of war with Mark because I did not understand his reluctance to do things my way. I took it as a challenge, and I believe he did the same in reverse. Now I know. People are wrapped up in their own lives and living into their own nature. When something seems irrational, it is often because we are using a different rationale. I have learned to put myself in their shoes and see what might be really happening for them. Another imperfect practice.

Everything is a Double-Edged Sword

I used to say that something was a double-edged sword, be it a person, an opportunity, a personality trait. Being a straight talker as I have been so dubbed, is a double-edged sword.

Early in my career that first job promotion was great, but it did not come with taking anything off my plate, just a heap more work. I was flattered by the promotion and eventually felt duped. Double-edged sword.

Mark's tendency to fix things means he wants to fix everything all the time. But sometimes, I only want a listening ear, especially since talking things out often leads me to the solution for myself. And what better way to feel accomplished than to take charge of my own life? I want to be my hero, and he wants to be my hero. Sometimes, what he really wants is to fix things so we can move on. He believes that because something is broken, fixing it is the solution, most especially emotions. Let's get those fixed right away with positive adages. I take the longer approach. I like to look for patterns and gain an understanding of how I got to a certain point. Marrying a fixer is a double-edged sword.

Nothing that comes with only one virtue. A new baby is a wonderful gift that wreaks havoc on your sleep. Freedom comes with responsibility. Enlightenment comes with a call to do better. Everything is a double-edged sword. If you can only see one edge, keep looking.

The Way You Start Your Day Defines Your Day

If you have ever read a self-help book, the author likely talks about a morning practice. I say so, too, because of the power it affords me. It will afford you the same.

Every day begins with me. Sometimes I go to the gym first, but then I sit somewhere quiet and write in my journal. Sometimes I write about my day ahead, sometimes about last night's dreams, sometimes about how yesterday turned out. Always about my feelings. It helps me to sort things out before I encounter others.

Next, I like to read something inspiring. It is a way to fill the soul. I love the book *A Deep Breath of Life* by Alan Cohen. Each day has a one page "food for thought" entry. It is uncanny how often whatever he wrote for that day has a personal meaning. You may choose to read the Bible or other devotional book that fills your soul, as long as you tend to the soul.

For outside counsel, I choose a card from an oracle deck. I have many to choose from so I use whichever inspires that day: Angels, Goddesses, Tarot, etc. Once I select the card, I read the definition in the little book, and – here's the important part – I put the date at the bottom of the page. Sometimes I will pull a card and say, "Oh, I've not had that before," and then I see that I had it three times in two months. Clearly, I am either not paying attention, or something is still an issue or unaddressed opportunity. I had a card not too long ago that I realized I have had once a year for three years in the same month and not any other time.

Then, the most challenging part of all, despite my incredible success in doing so, I sit in the silence for at least ten minutes. It will blow you away! Not every day but often enough. As one practitioner told me, it is like making a date with Spirit. Spirit knows when you will be still and ready to receive, it is easier to communicate. Sometimes I use guided meditation to check in with my chakras. I love doing this because it is a great way for me to know what belongs to me before encountering others. If I know I did not have that twinge in my gut before I came to this meeting, but I have it now, I know it does not belong to me and to pay attention to others who may feel their power is being challenged or are about to challenge my power.

In my morning practice, I can write for many pages or half a page. I can meditate for ten minutes or thirty or more, depending on what is happening for me. What I can tell you above all else is this:

- When I start my day with me, the rest of the world seems more obvious and separate from whatever I am experiencing. Taking life less personally is a true gift.
- Tending to my feelings, my soul, and Spirit everyday lead to a greater sense of calm and possibility.
- When I am loyal to my morning practice, I have more patience with Mark and the rest of the world. It allows me to be more considerate because the more in tune I am with my world, the easier to see them acting in response to their world.

My son came home from elementary school one day, distraught at how mean his teacher had been. He reported she yelled at little things anyone did, and it really upset him. I offered that it sounds like something else was bothering her. Maybe she had a fight with her husband or something in her personal life was not going well. He was so relieved. It had not dawned on him that it was not something he had done nor could he change by behaving differently. Considering that the teacher was having a day that was not in response to him was so clarifying. He told me years later how that thought helped him with future situations. It is important to know what yours is, and what is not as you go throughout the day. That is why I encourage all of my clients to have a morning practice. Becoming more aware of me has led me to become more effective in my life, with clients' situations, and especially with my loved ones. I stress a morning practice because it starts the day off with set intentions versus the end of day when it tends to be hindsight. (Although on occasion, I also journal in the evening to review and unload.)

Exercise 8:

1. Note in your journal where you might be spending time looking for external validation. When you find it, what does it add to your understanding of yourself? When it is not forthcoming, how much time do you spend continuing to pursue it? Find where you are being held captive and how you might free yourself.

2. Begin a morning practice. Include journaling, a simple inspirational reading, and sitting in the silence for ten minutes. Many resist this because they don't have the time. I counter

that all the time and energy used later in the day that burns you out could be avoided with this upfront time. Not being aware of yourself costs you. Being more aware of yourself saves you.

Mary Flanagan Gleason

AN INVITATION

There is no such thing as getting to the other side and now everything is fine. It is more that each lesson and story of survival comes with more tools to employ in the future. The next wave is always coming. Some are gentle, and some are overpowering. Swimming at the Jersey shore, I learned there are a few ways to handle waves. One is to stand your ground, get overwhelmed, and be violently delivered to the shore. Or you can jump up to catch the wave. When you jump up, the wave will either gently rock you for a moment as it passes by or lift you and more gently deliver you to the shore. If I see each new challenge as a temporary, fleeting wave, I look for ways to jump up and catch a ride. I may not always want to go to the shore but at least I will arrive with greater calm and grace. Of course, I cannot always see the next wave coming. Sometimes I get pushed over and end up feeling pushed around. But I know now, more so than ever before, that I will figure it out. The wave will ebb. This, too, shall pass.

If you have found even one element in this book that rings true for you, or if you have recognized another person you care about and can look at them with fresh eyes, or if you found this book amusing or otherwise worth reading, this was a worthwhile endeavor. If you feel like you want to know more, I am always happy to hear from you.

Most of all, I welcome you to my community, which I build with intention and fill with grace. Being an intuitive and using your intuition is a gift, and I hope you will embrace yours, be you a woo woo or an engineer.

Cheers to an imperfect life lived full out. May your lessons be learned and your time in this life lead you to greater prosperity.

"To be nobody but yourself in a world which is doing its best, night and day, to make you everybody else, means to fight the hardest battle which any human being can fight; and never stop fighting."
— e. e. cummings

APPENDIX A

Affirmations

Your thoughts are the most powerful force of energy and key to whatever you wish to manifest. The secret to effective affirmations is to voice them as if they are already true. "I will make good decisions" means that is forever somewhere in the future. "I make good decisions" allows you to live into that reality now. One more thing, the subconscious hears only positives. "I don't want to make bad decisions" becomes "I want to make bad decisions." Keep your thoughts and your affirmations positive. My favorite one is "Money flows to me easily and often." Here are a few more to start you off. Add or modify as you go.

- My intuition is my one true barometer. I honor it by checking in with it.
- My intuition is a valuable part of my decision making.
- I honor both sides of my brain.
- When something is right, I know and trust it.
- When something is wrong, I know and trust it.
- My intuition is as valuable as data. I give it equal weight in decisions.
- I am powerful beyond all measure.

- All that flows to me is for my greatest good and highest purpose.
- Where there is light, there is truth.
- Everything I have visualized, intended, prayed about and worked for is already on its way to me.
- I allow others to have their experiences as I honor my own.
- I am here to be a blessing. I trust Spirit with the details.
- Every day is a color. Today I pick the color _____ and live in its vibration.
- All that I need is provided to me. I live in abundance.
- I change my world by changing my thoughts.

BIBLIOGRAPHY

Bach, Richard- *Jonathan Livingston Seagull* MacMillan Publishers 1970

Bloom, Kristina- *Intuitive You! Psychic and Personal Development* Moonbow Publications, 2020

Bolte Taylor- Dr. Jill- *My Stroke of Insight* Viking 2008

Capra, Fritja- *The Tao of Physics: An Exploration of the Parallels Between Modern Physics and Eastern Mysticism* Shambhala Publications, Inc. 1983

Chapman, Gary- *The Five Love Languages: How to Express Heartfelt Commitment to Your Mate* Northfield Publishing, 1992, 1995, 2004, 2010

Cohen, Alan- *A Deep Breath of Life: Daily Inspiration for Heart-Centered Living* Hay House 1996 Northfield Publishing 2010

Daniels, Dr. David and Dr. Virginia Price- *Essential Enneagram: The Definitive Personality Test and Self-Discovery Guide* Harper One 2000

Dispenza, Joe Dr.- *You Are the Placebo* Hay House 2014

Hay, Louise- *Heal Your Body: The Mental Causes of Physical Illness and Metaphysical Ways to Overcome Them.* Hay House 1982, 2008

Judith, Dr. Anodea- *Wheels of Life* Llewellyn Worldwide 1999

Kasanoff, Bruce- Intuition is the highest form of intelligence-Forbes.com website, Feb 2017

Lipton, Dr. Bruce H.- *The Biology of Belief* Hay House, Inc., 2015

Briggs Myers, Isabel and Katharine Cook Briggs- "The Myers Briggs Type Indicator (MBTI)" Refer to myersbriggs.org website.

Olson, Jeffrey G- *The Slight Edge* Success Books 2011

O'Rouke, Jack- *The Rational Psychic*: A Skeptic's Guide to Extraordina Perception Sounds True 2012

Pond, David- *Chakras for Beginners* Llewellyn Publications 2000

Redfield, James- *The Celestine Prophecy* Grand Central Publishing 1993

Schucman, Helen- *A Course in Miracles* Circle of Atonement, 2017

What the Bleep Do We Know!?, movie edited by Jonathon Shaw 2004

Made in the USA
Las Vegas, NV
04 December 2021

36069814R00105